All God's Children

Philadelphia Mennonites of Lancaster Conference

1899 - 1999

by

Jeff Gingerich and Miriam Stoltzfus

Photos on front cover

Top row of three photos left to right:
    Alma Ruth and Emma Rudy
    J. Paul Graybill
    Clinton and Maybelle Ferster

Middle group photo:
    Philadelphia Leadership - January 1999
    Philadelphia, Pennsylvania
1st row seated l to r:
    Bishop Freeman Miller, Bishop Emeritus Luke Stoltzfus, Miriam Stoltzfus,
    Nadine Smith-Bulford, Pam Royster
2nd row l to r:
    Truong Tu, Sarin Lay, Polly Alcantara, Oscar Dungan, Leonard Burkholder
Back row l to r:
    Dwayne Royster, Richard Hwang, Tuyen Nguyen, Leonard Dow,
    Otis Banks, Lemuel So, Sing Kin So, Ron Sider, Charles Bulford

Bottom two photos left to right:
    Barbara Herr
    John Winters

All God's Children
Philadelphia Mennonites of Lancaster Conference
1899 - 1999

by
Jeff Gingerich and Miriam Stoltzfus

ISBN 0-9661907-4-2

Printed in USA
Imperial Graphics
P.O. Box 340, Leola, Pennsylvania 17540

Preface

It's a pleasure to be able to introduce this new history of Philadelphia Mennonite churches, which I have read with much enjoyment and great appreciation.

When, as a new Christian – and a sailor – I first visited one of those churches – Norris Square – in 1966, I was made to feel welcome enough to keep coming back. Despite its commitment to non-resistance, at Norris Square Mennonite Church, all God's children included me. I enjoyed not only its hospitality, but its nurturing environment. Both took place, not just on Sunday mornings and evenings at the church building however, but also in homes and on the streets. The homes were principally those of Jacob and Anna Frederick and most regularly, Galen and Janice Martin, with whom two 1-W's (conscientious objectors serving in Philadelphia), Linford Martin and Donny Lehman lived. The streets were those upon which we delivered *The Way*, a publication designed to introduce people to the Faith and our church. These, together with Fred Yocum's Sunday school class, started me on my way in the Mennonite Church

I entered the navy during the Vietnam War era, about a year and a half after graduating from high school. By the time I came to Norris Square, I had completed 30 hours of college credits and was anticipating entering the naval academy (I had just been nominated by one of the congressmen in my home state and anticipated an appointment for the spring. More and more, however, I had felt led in the direction of the ministry, and the persistent encouragement of friends at Norris Square, Oxford Circle and Diamond Street to consider Eastern Mennonite College finally persuaded me to forsake the open door in Troas (Annapolis) for Macedonia (Harrisonburg).

Two pastors of Norris Square had a great influence on my spiritual growth – Jacob Frederick, the pastor, and Clarence Fretz, who was now living in Maryland. When Clarence heard that there was a young sailor attending Norris Square, he began writing to me with all sorts of questions and advice – advice that extended, eventually, to suggestions for dates and inquiries about other dates! With mentors like Clarence and Jacob, and a supportive new network of friends, it was not difficult to pin down and follow my life's direction.

I have retained and cherished those early friendships over the years. They have often served as a model for me in relating to other novices in the Faith. In those days, many Mennonites were skeptical of establishing city churches – too many bad influences. I, for one, am glad someone had a vision for a role for Mennonites in Philadelphia – one that included Norris Square Mennonite Church

> – *Art McPhee*
> *Professor,*
> *Associated Mennonite Biblical Seminaries*

Introduction

All God's Children includes the stories of persons over the last 100 years following their call from the Lord to bring the saving knowledge of the Gospel to the people of Philadelphia. The Mennonites came from Europe to the port of Philadelphia in 1683 looking for freedom of worship and settling in Germantown.

Philadelphia developed with communities of similar languages, cultures, economic status, religions, and races. Mennonites soon settled into farming communities to the north and west, and marketed their farm products in the city. In the 1890's, a missionary conviction was developing among these persons.

The story unfolds showing the cooperation of Franconia and Lancaster Conferences, and Eastern Mennonite Mission (EMM). The Germanic Mennonites did not always understand the heartbeat of persons so different from themselves. The emphasis on church discipline was not easily accepted. There were only a few families that remained Mennonite for successive generations. Interpretation of convictions and church directives were sincere for their time periods. The Word of God as it was planted in many hearts has yielded fruit in unexpected places and continues to challenge each of us to a faithful walk in service for the Lord.

You will read about persons who had a real dedication to serve their Lord and gave themselves in various types of service. There were those who served their lifetime and those who served for shorter periods enabling many avenues for the spread of the Gospel. Missionary Training Institute, a teaching program of Eastern Mennonite Board of Missions and Charities, broadened the city ministry and taught skills for witnessing to a large number of persons in the broader church constituency.

There was always a strong emphasis on the Word of God. Bible Memory work in the Sunday School, Bible School, Children's Church time, street evangelism, and boys' and girls' clubs were fundamental activities. Bible Study and Prayer Time were foundational for strength and vision.

Our hope is that this book may not only be a record. Seeing the challenges of the Word of God being fulfilled has strengthened both those who served and the recipients. Together the kingdom of God has grown and the vision for the church of the future has enlarged. The church that began with two Sister Workers as the first missionaries grew into churches of many ethnic groups and languages. This is a story that needs to be told. Reviewing the past while anticipating the future helps us gain perspective. Possibly some may want to use this book for mission studies and/or church planting insights.

> *- Jacob and Anna Frederick*
> (former Philadelphia Mennonite
> church workers)

Acknowledgements

The creation of this book was truly a collaborative effort. The idea first germinated in a group of present and former Lancaster Conference Mennonite church leaders who got together to form the Philadelphia Mennonite Historical Committee in 1998. The inspiration for the committee was the upcoming 100-year anniversary of Lancaster Conference's involvement in Philadelphia. The committee's core members, consisting of Anna and Jacob Frederick, Raymond Jackson, Freeman Miller, Mattie Nikiema, and Miriam and Luke Stoltzfus, met together periodically for two years as the book was slowly pieced together. They were joined by Jeff Gingerich, a graduate student at the University of Pennsylvania, shortly after the committee was formed. Carolyn Charles Wenger and Allen Brubaker also attended meetings when their schedules allowed. During the formation of the book we have been blessed by contributions of letters, stories, and photographs from people who have had involvement with the Philadelphia Mennonite Church. We are extremely grateful for these gifts of memories and stored-away documents that have been submitted.

Much of this history had already been documented and we admittedly borrowed liberally from this previously written material. We have tried as much as possible to give credit whenever we have done so, and have obtained permission from all of these sources. The Tom Fitch story, as told in the Introduction, was originally written by Kathleen Hayes in *The Mennonite*. In 1986, Ross Bender wrote an article on the 1st and 2nd Mennonite Churches of Philadelphia[1] that was helpful to the introductory section. Information on the "sister workers" at the Norris Square and Diamond Street congregations was excerpted from a 1989 article written by A. Grace Wenger in *The Missionary Messenger*[2]. In detailing the story of the Diamond Street Mennonite Congregation, excerpts were borrowed from a 1995 article written by Robert Good in the *Pennsylvania Mennonite Heritage*[3]. In 1993, an article written by David Greiser was published in the *Gospel Herald*[4] about all of the Mennonite Churches in Philadelphia and this was very helpful to us in our writing.

Some of the material was originally written and submitted by individuals other than those named as authors, although we have edited these pieces for the book. Jacob and Anna Frederick wrote the introduction to the book and contributed greatly to the Norris Square and Oxford Circle sections. John Winters and Jim Leaman contributed to the Oxford Circle section through personal correspondence. Jim also was largely responsible for the Jewish Witness section of the book. Margaret Allen originally wrote the sidebar on the Bethany Childcare Center. Vanna and Peter Lay of the Philadelphia Cambodian Mennonite Church, Ton Alcantara of Kapitaran Christian Fellowship, Charles and Nadine Smith-Bulford of New Mercies Mennonite Church, and Duane and Pam Royster of Way of Life Church each wrote the majority of the sections for their respective churches. We appreciate the contribution of the other pastors who provided information through interviews and editing. We are also grateful to Arbutus Sider for writing the history of the Philadelphia Mennonite High School, and to Bishop Freeman Miller for concluding the book with a look to the future.

Finally, we want to express our appreciation to the staff at Lancaster Mennonite Historical Society and Eastern Mennonite Missions for their financial contribution to the publishing of this book, and to Jim Stoner and staff at Imperial Graphics for their excellent work in the layout and publishing of the book.

Philadelphia Mennonite Churches

– Neighborhoods of Philadelphia –

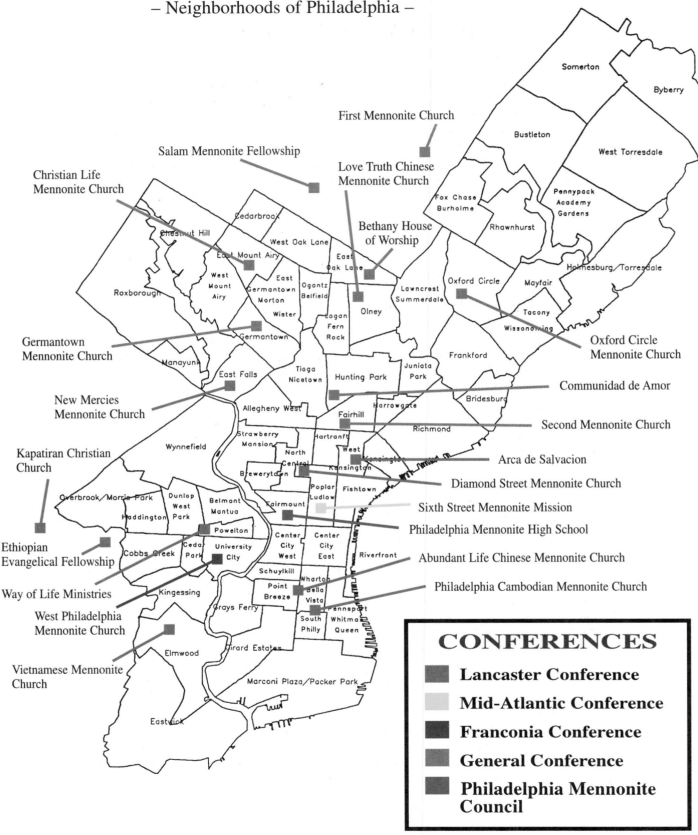

First Mennonite Church

Salam Mennonite Fellowship

Love Truth Chinese
Mennonite Church

Christian Life
Mennonite Church

Bethany House
of Worship

Germantown
Mennonite Church

Oxford Circle
Mennonite Church

New Mercies
Mennonite Church

Communidad de Amor

Second Mennonite Church

Kapatiran Christian
Church

Arca de Salvacion

Diamond Street Mennonite Church

Sixth Street Mennonite Mission

Philadelphia Mennonite High School

Ethiopian
Evangelical Fellowship

Abundant Life Chinese Mennonite Church

Way of Life Ministries

Philadelphia Cambodian Mennonite Church

West Philadelphia
Mennonite Church

Vietnamese Mennonite
Church

CONFERENCES

- Lancaster Conference
- Mid-Atlantic Conference
- Franconia Conference
- General Conference
- Philadelphia Mennonite Council

Table of Contents

The Story of Tom Fitch

He could play gospel music like the best of them. He exuded joy not only with his fingers, but with his whole body. He didn't just sit on the piano bench and play; he bounced around so much that it seemed a miracle he could keep his fingers on the right keys. When Tom Fitch played gospel music, you couldn't help but catch the Spirit.

After putting his faith in Christ and experiencing true love and joy, he joined his college's black gospel choir in Berkeley, California with some trepidation, wondering how he would be accepted, since there were no other whites in the group. Tom wrote, " But I heard them singing about Jesus in a way that touched me deeply, and that gave me courage to believe I might somehow belong with them. What a delight to be warmly welcomed as a brother in Christ! I felt so privileged and joyful to sing and pray and move with them".

When he moved to Philadelphia to study music at Temple University Graduate School in 1979, he soon discovered nearby Diamond Street Mennonite Church, an integrated congregation of African-Americans and whites, plus some Africans, Palestinians and a few other internationals. The worship style reflected the African-American neighborhood where it was situated. "We had just lost a gifted choir director and were praying for a new one," Freeman Miller, then pastor at Diamond Street, comments, "but we could never have dreamed up Tom Fitch; he was God's creation. On his very first Sunday visiting the church, he played 'God Has Smiled on Me' on that little piano squeezed into the front corner, and Diamond Street Mennonite Church changed forever. There was instant electricity across the room".

The interracial choir thrived under Tom's leadership. Besides growing in number and ability, they made two cassette tapes (still available through the church), toured throughout the United States and Canada and sang at the Mennonite World Conference assembly in Strasbourg, France, in 1984. Wherever they went, their message was to allow the love of Christ to break down racial barriers and build unity in Him. When the struggling church could not afford to pay Tom enough to support his family, he served with Mennonite Voluntary Service for several years, overseeing the construction of the Diamond Street Community Center gymnasium. In 1990, Tom and his family moved to Minneapolis, Minnesota to become the full-time music director of Park Avenue Methodist, a 1200-member congregation that is about 65% white and 35% people of color.

Tom had always loved music, but through his Christian faith, music had a clear purpose: sharing the message that God loves all peo-

Diamond Street Mennonite Church Choir
front row l to r: Tom Fitch, Bea (Grimes) Macon, Janelle Gingerich, Sue (Rutt) Glick, Sharon Gabriel, Marie Clemens, Fred Clemens, Mattie (Cooper) Nikiema, Wanda Bryant, Walter Baynard, Tim Baynard, Ron Vessels, Mark Lopez, Dan Heebner, William Jackson, Charles Baynard, Carlos Jones, Henry Blocker, Art Griffin

ple and wants us all to love one another as one body, regardless of race and ethnicity. Tom's dedication to Christ's message of reconciliation was as contagious as his love for music. And he lived it wholeheartedly. He brought together the rich and the poor, black and white, Israeli and Palestinian, American and African, even city

folks and country folks. Tom knew God's love for him, after many years of searching, and desperately wanted others to experience that love, too.

Tom died of cancer in November of 1997. Special memorial services were held at Diamond Street Mennonite Church on February 8th, 1998. An offering of $2300 was given to Tom's wife, Rebecca, for the family. She promptly gave this back to the church for the completion of the community center's gymnasium. At the memorial service, Pastor Otis Banks honored Tom by naming the gym the Tom Fitch Memorial Gymnasium. One of the recordings of the Diamond Street Gospel Choir led by T___ was titled "All God's Children", an inspiration for the title of this book.

The Tom Fitch Family
Rebecca (Ryman), Tom, Micah, Mari and Aaron

Philadelphia Mennonites - The Early Years

The involvement of the Mennonite Church's Lancaster Conference in the city of Philadelphia was initially a reluctant step forward. Church leaders in Lancaster were unsure as to whether they should support the vision of mission work in the nearby big city, or whether they should concentrate their efforts on solidifying the community of believers back home. Eventually, the increasing fervor of a call to the Great Commission won out and institutional support was given to urban mission efforts, but not before a few Mennonites had already begun their work in Philadelphia. We begin by briefly summarizing this prior Mennonite church work in Philadelphia and setting the Lancaster Conference efforts within the context of the larger religious landscape in the United States at the time.

The first Mennonites to arrive in the United States settled in the area surrounding the historic and economically thriving metropolis of Philadelphia in 1683. Many of them settled in the area now known as Germantown, a town seven miles northwest of Philadelphia (now a part of the city limits) and some moved to the farming communities of Franconia and Lancaster[5]. It is not likely that this small community of German Anabaptists had envisioned that some day, three centuries later, a thriving community of twenty-two congregations would be established in the Philadelphia area with a representation of a variety of ethnic groups, worshiping in eleven different languages, and all calling themselves Mennonite.

These Germantown settlers built a meetinghouse in the area and this building housed the Germantown Mennonite church for over three hundred years until 1993 when the congregation outgrew the historic building on Germantown Avenue and moved to a larger building on Washington Lane (about two blocks from the former location). In an 1847 division in the Franconia Conference of the Mennonite Church, the small congregation in Germantown sided with those who left the Franconia Conference, and became a part of the Eastern District of the General Conference Mennonite Church. Today, this congregation continues to worship together each Sunday morning as descendents of the original American Mennonites.

As many Anabaptist immigrants came through the port of Philadelphia, they settled on the rich farmland in the surrounding counties. Others found employment in the city. Those on the surrounding farms needed a market to sell their produce. This they found in the city. Their interaction with the city dwellers brought a concern for the spiritual welfare of their customers.

The Eastern District of the General Conference Mennonite Church became involved in the city of Philadelphia in the latter part of the 19th century. In 1862, Daniel Hege, while collecting donations for a Mennonite seminary, visited families in Philadelphia who had retained membership in country churches. As a result of discussion with these families and a vision for church growth, Hege suggested that there were enough Mennonites in Philadelphia to support their own church and soon, with the assistance of the General Conference Mennonite Church, services were begun in member's homes. In 1865 a chapel was rented and in 1881 a brick building was built at Reese and Diamond Streets. During the pastorate of Nathaniel B. Grubb (1882 - 1921), First Mennonite experienced a period of rapid growth, reaching as high as 484 members in 1928.

Nathaniel Grubb had a passion for church-planting and subsequently Second Mennonite of Philadelphia was planted at the corner of Franklin and Indiana Streets (about 1 mile from the mother church) in 1899 with Grubb's son Silas as the first pastor. This church has remained at the same location, having adapted to the changing racial demographics of the neighborhood by providing African-American leadership in the pulpit. After many years of devoted leadership to the church, Carlton Minnis retired, and the congregation is now pastored by Darryl Wallace. First Mennonite eventually purchased property in Huntingdon Valley and built a church building in 1959 as a result of the loss of membership to the suburbs[6].

Subsequently, when Mennonites from the Lancaster Conference began to envision mission work in the city, they had role models from within the denomination to follow. But there was very little interaction between the General Conference and Mennonite Church Conference during this era. Mennonites in other areas of the country were also catching the spirit of evangelistic mission work at this time. In Chicago, the 1893 World's Fair spurred the work of

Tom and Jean Hunsberger, Rev. Carlton and Hattie Minnis, Sister Barbara Wallace, Rev. Darryl Wallace holding Justin with other church children, at Second Mennonite Church, 1999.

young Mennonite idealists to begin missionary work in the city. Later, the work of James and Rowena Lark, the first African-American Mennonite Bishop, became well-known throughout the church[7]. The Mennonite church's passage into the 20th century was one of renewed evangelical outreach to both foreign countries and urban America, requiring Mennonite church leaders to rethink the traditional structures of their organizations, and to envision a possible new identity for Mennonites in the United States. The Lancaster Conference, known as one of the most conservative conferences, was being watched closely for the changes that these new ideas and structures might bring. Other Mennonites were interested to see how these new types of outreaches would affect the traditions to which the conference adhered.

Similar changes were taking place in the broader U.S. religious landscape. The turn of the nineteenth century heralded the influx of European immigrants, bringing with them an ethnic and religious pluralism that would dramatically alter the structure of the most dominant Protestant religious groups of that time. From 1891 to 1900, the number of immigrants to the United States totaled 3,687,564. This rose to 8,795,386 in the decade between 1901 and 1910[8]. Most of these immigrants brought strong ties to their cultural and religious church traditions, yet this was accompanied by the desire to appropriate their old culture into the life and ideals of their new homeland. As a result, the demographic landscape that early Lancaster Conference missionaries encountered when they arrived in Philadelphia was a diverse number of immigrant neighborhoods, tight ethnic enclaves where individuals found communal support. Although residential segregation by race was not as apparent as in other parts of the country, social segregation by race was still strongly enforced. Lancaster Conference missionaries involved themselves first in the European immigrant neighborhoods, where some of these Mennonites already had ties through their business activities.

As we will see, much of the work of Lancaster Conference Mennonites in Philadelphia throughout the first part of the twentieth century was the work of women. These women were called "sister workers" and although they were not given official leadership positions in the church at the time, they provided the foundation for church structure and developed neighborhood relationships that sustained the early mission efforts during these first years. This phenomenon was not unique to the Philadelphia mission work. Juhnke[9] notes that: "For Mennonite women, missions created and won approval for new religious roles...single women assumed responsibilities and status far beyond what church and society were likely to allow them at home". While male pastors would come and go, the sister workers provided a long-term, relational presence that provided stability for the work of growing a church in Philadelphia.

In this first section, the story will be told of the growth of the three oldest Lancaster Conference churches in Philadelphia. It is a story of a small mission turning into an established congregation (Norris Square), which subsequently branched off two additional congregations, one as a result of the fears of racial integration (Diamond Street), and the other in an effort to reach a poor white community in another part of the city (Oxford Circle). It is the story of the sowing of seeds in preparation for the growth of the thirteen churches that emerged later on in the century.

Norris Square Mennonite Church

Joseph Bleam Bechtel (1856 - 1928)
Catharine Bertolet Diehl (1875 - 1974)

June of 1899 can be considered the beginning of the now century-long involvement of the Lancaster Conference in the city of Philadelphia. It was during this month that a mission in Philadelphia was begun by members of the Mennonite Church[10] from both the Franconia and Lancaster Conferences. In a city where Mennonites had occasionally shopped and marketed their goods, mission was a unique phenomenon.

Isaac Kulp of Bucks County and Joseph Bechtel of Berks County most likely did not set out to be church planters. Kulp, a grocery store owner, and Bechtel, a building contractor, both moved to Philadelphia in the 1890's for occupational reasons but began to develop a concern for their neighbors in the city. The neighborhood that they decided to focus their attention on was known as Kensington. It was the home of a variety of European ethnic groups who came to Philadelphia to work on the ports or in one of the many textile factories in the area. It was a bustling area with many different languages heard on the streets. Saloons could be found on most corners. The cobblestone streets were filled with activity, much of which Kulp and Bechtel must have considered quite ungodly at the time. The area was also heavily Roman Catholic.

Kulp and Bechtel met with the leadership of Franconia Conference where there was little interest in officially sponsoring a Philadelphia mission, although they ruled that individuals were free to make "any contribution to the mission"[11]. They next turned to the Mennonites of Lancaster Conference. Here they found a group called the Mennonite Sunday School Mission (now known as Eastern Mennonite Missions) who were willing to give them support. Enough money was granted to rent a house at 1930 East York Street in the Kensington area and support a couple of live-in mission workers. Although little is known of the immediate reaction of people in the surrounding neighborhood, the Mennonites in their plain clothes must have been a curious sight when they moved into the community. The work began under difficult circumstances. The Franconia and Lancaster bishop boards would neither sanction nor forbid the operation of the mission. Both boards allowed their ministers to visit the Philadelphia mission, but gave them strict orders to conduct services in the same way "like those held at home". Few workers wanted to pursue such activity very long.

Amanda Musselman
(1870 - 1940)

The Philadelphia Mennonite Mission, as it was originally called, was opened by two dedicated women who each gave twenty-five years of their lives to the work in Philadelphia. The names of Mary Denlinger and Amanda Musselman were almost synonymous with the Mennonite Mission for the first two decades, and "Sister Amanda" and "Sister Mary" were spoken together almost as one[12]. Mary Denlinger was from

Paradise, Pennsylvania where she taught in a mission-minded Sunday School. She went to the Chicago Home Mission in 1884 as a voluntary worker. Her experiences there prepared her for the work in Philadelphia. Amanda Musselman was from the Groffdale Mennonite Church near New Holland. She was invited to serve at the Philadelphia Mission before it opened. In the winter of 1899, she went to Chicago to become familiar with home mission work. That was the beginning of her friendship with Mary Denlinger that lasted until Amanda's death in 1940.

The two women left Chicago in 1899 to begin the Philadelphia Mission. They moved into what Amanda described as a "dirty, greasy, bedbug house" at 1930 East York Street. They cleaned and furnished the house with second-hand furniture, but even before everything was in order, their mission work began. Mary later recalled that, "Canvassing the district, we found some people kind while others closed the door against us, and we wondered if we could ever have a Sunday School. But thank God, on Lord's day morning, June 11, 1899, all was in readiness and we had a meeting with about 20 people"[13]. Only one of those present, a child, was from the neighborhood. The rest were Mennonites from outside of the city. The first preaching service took place in July, with Daniel Kauffman preaching the first sermon.

On their second Sunday in Philadelphia, the sisters began visitation. This became a significant part of the outreach. Amanda wrote, "It (housing) was much like many we visited in Chicago, wretched in every way." Sewing school on

(1892 - 1949)

Saturdays began a few weeks later with only five girls at the first class. Before long the group grew, and soon the neighborhood girls were making nightgowns, skirts, and winter underwear, accomplishments that pleased their mothers greatly. Activities at the mission soon fell into a pattern: Sunday School on Sunday morning, children's meeting and Bible study on Sunday evening; Bible study on Tuesday evening; memory work on Thursday evening; and sewing school on Saturday.

Among the first children to attend Sunday School was Harriet Sanderson. She and five others from her family became members twenty-eight years later. Another eager pupil was eight-year old May Gauger who held perfect attendance in Sunday School that first year. When May grew up, she became a faithful member who taught Sunday School for many years and kept neat and accurate records of the services. When May wanted to be baptized and dress like the sister workers, Mary and

Sister May S. Gauger
- obituary written by J. Paul Graybill

May S. Gauger, 1936 E. York Street, Philadelphia was born February 29, 1892, died from the same residence on March 30, 1949, 57 years, 1 month, and 1 day. Sister May, as she was commonly called, endeared herself to many church friends and also to a large circle of neighbors and business friends. She was present as a little girl on the 2nd Sunday of the opening of the Mennonite Mission of Philadelphia at 1930 E. York Street, the 3rd door from her home. She was baptized as a member of the Mission congregation in December, 1912, although hindered by her parents in doing so. She was a stenographer and worked for a number of years in the office of Hires-Turner Glass Company. Sister May had the unusual combination of mental ability, strong personality, coupled with devotion to the Lord and a loyalty to the church. She was an able teacher in the Mission Sunday School for many years until her health failed. She had a strong influence in a large circle of friends.

Amanda, her German Lutheran parents denied her wishes, saying they would disinherit her if she would become a Mennonite. She honored her parents' wishes and gave them loving care during their aging years until their deaths. They designated that their home at 1936 East York St. (three doors from the mission) would be May's as long as she needed it. May later became a member and, before her own death, indicated that the property was to become her brother William's, and at his death it was to become the inheritance of Eastern Mennonite Missions. After William's death, the property was renovated and was used for housing by various people who were assisting with the work of the Philadelphia Churches[14].

By 1902, the sister workers had moved to another rented house at the corner of Dauphin and Amber because they were attracting more and more people to their services. For several years, ministers came from Franconia

Conference to preach on alternate Sunday afternoons, traveling to the city by train or trolley after they had conducted services in their home churches in the country.

In 1907, the Lancaster County Sunday School Mission Board, with significant donations from the Franconia Conference, purchased a large 14-room building at 2151 North Howard Street that faced a park called Norris Square. That same year, Lancaster Conference also began to send a preacher every two weeks so that there was preaching every Sunday afternoon with an evening service when it was convenient for the preacher to stay overnight. Others who helped in those years were Jacob Buckwalter who traveled by train, trolley, or steamboat from Wilmington, Delaware, J.D. and Hettie (Kulp) Mininger, and Joseph Bechtel who held the office of Sunday School superintendent from the beginning until his death in 1928.

Harriet Sanderson and mother Mary

The sisters did their best to work with those who suffered with poverty and alienation from their home country, taking food, clothing and fuel to needy families. Sometimes they used their own money to help in this work. Friends from the country also sent in provisions, supplies for Sunday School, furniture and equipment for the mission home, and food for the poor, especially at Christmas and Thanksgiving.

In 1922, Paul and Phebe Graybill, a young couple from New Holland who had sensed the missionary call, were sent to the Philadelphia Mission. Paul was to become superintendent. This signified a clear sanction from the Lancaster Conference to continue this urban work. Paul, young and innovative, introduced outdoor song services, Summer Bible School, and evangelistic tent meetings. He was indeed a "progressive conservative": progressive with new ideas, a vision for mission, and strong on education; and conservative on the authority of the church, teaching by indoctrination and nonconformity to the world through rigid dress standards[15]. The progressive mission impulse, which he espoused, by its nature needed to break down certain walls to the outside world, while the conservative dress standards by their nature tended to bolster and maintain those walls. As an example of this dilemma, the Sunday School in Philadelphia grew rapidly under Graybill's leadership, but growth in church membership did not automatically follow. During the years of his ministry, only about a third of those who entered the applicant's classes actually became members. It seems that the austere standards of dress demanded a social courage that few were ready to embrace.

The sister workers experienced difficulty in working with the young couple, even though Amanda was Phebe's aunt. After spending nearly twenty-five years in devoted labor, the sisters found it hard to surrender leadership to a younger man such as Graybill who had been told by his bishop to maintain control over the mission work. With characteristic loyalty to the church, none of those involved ever revealed the underlying nature of the problem. Because of the disagreements, Paul and Phebe left the mission for nearly a year in 1923.

Amanda Musselman and Mary Denlinger departed permanently from the Mission in July 1924. The Graybills returned to Philadelphia in August of that same year. In September, some sixty people of the community signed a petition requesting the return of Sisters Amanda and Mary, which read in part: "There is work that can never be done unless they come back and their work which is unfinished at the present time cannot be successfully taken up. They have proven themselves earnest and true workers for

Jacob S. and Fannie (Eberly) Buckwalter in Bible Class ca. 1946

the Lord and through their untiring efforts have drawn many people to the Mission"[16]. Despite this fervent request to come back to the city, the two sister workers did not return and spent the remainder of their retirement in Lancaster County.

Most of the mission work between 1907 and 1930 consisted of the weekly activities of Sunday School, preaching, Bible study, and sewing school for the girls. During the summer of 1927, Graybill began to initiate a series of gospel meetings and summer Bible school classes in the Norris Square Park vicinity. These meetings were new types of ministry for Mennonites and were closely watched and reported on by Lancaster church leaders[17]. Around 100 people attended the gospel meetings. By 1931, he began a series of winter Bible schools. The Bible School was to become a consistent feature of the Norris Square congregation for years to come.

Around 1925, a little girl named Mary Bromley, age seven, was attending the Mission sewing school and Sunday school. After attending for a while she expressed desire

Naomi, Paul, Jr., J. Paul and Phebe Graybill, Huldah, Anna Lois

Mary Denlinger: Sister Worker

(1867 - 1958)

"She stands out in my memory for her quiet and contented spirit which can be shown in two of the phrases I often heard her say. Of the weather, she would say, 'When the Lord sorts out the weather and sends rain, then rain's my choice.' The other is a phrase attributed to her concerning her death, 'I'm going up higher'".

- *Miriam R.(Weaver) Stoltzfus*

to dress like her teacher. Because she was so young, the matter of instruction and church membership was dropped for some time. But as time went on she made several expressions that showed she wanted to join the church and become a Christian. Her grandfather, James Bromley, who lived with the family and who had not attended church for many years, at times would bring the little girl to Sunday School. Then he would go to the square across from the mission and read the newspaper until Sunday School was dismissed. After repeated efforts, the little girl finally succeeded in getting her grandfather into the men's class. After attending Sunday School for a while, he began coming for the evening service, and then the afternoon service, and later even the midweek service. He wanted to know how to be "born again". Soon, he and Mary and a number of others received instruction preparatory for church membership.

Plush Hill Hangout
R.R.R.G.
Phila SEP 1 1926

Brother Hershey
Mennonite Mission

Dear Brother
I have just returned from my vacation at Atlantic city and on returning home I am informed that you have not moved out as requested. You must not care much for your life or you would not defy us by keeping your mission in its present location. This

is your last warning. we will give you a week to move. Remember we are watching and a few of your comrades very closely so don't trying talking the police. We just wanted your mission moved to a different locality not less than 15 blocks away from its present place. Enough.
Yours dishonorably.
Imperial Wizard R.R.R.

I WEEK
SEP 1 1926
TO
SEP 8 1926

REMEMBER
THE
"BLACK
SPOT"

Letter from the RRR Gang - 1926

Some weeks later Mary's father, Joseph Bromley, was invited to attend Sunday School. The next day Mary, eight years old, asked Graybill to visit her parents as they wanted to be Christians, too. The parents had not attended church nor cared for it for some years. Joseph Bromley was much more interested in sports. In the fall of 1926, he had broken his arm in a football game. Through Mary, the Mission found out that he was out of

First Tent Bible School - 1927
John F. Bressler in back on the left

work because of the accident. So when Mary said her parents wanted instruction, Graybill went to investigate. The mother had never been to the Mission, and the father had attended only once. Joseph Bromley said he changed his attitude to spiritual things for two reasons. First were the many questions that little Mary asked which they could not answer. And second was the kindness of the Mission folks in giving them help when they were in need. They continued in Bible study and in instruction for church membership. The four Bromleys and ten others were baptized in the spring of 1927. Joseph Bromley continued faithfully through the years, teaching Sunday School, and becoming Sunday School Superintendent as well[18]. He was ordained as Deacon of the church in 1939.

As when the Mission began, sister workers continued to play a significant role in the ongoing mission work. In 1926, two years after Sisters Mary Denlinger and Amanda Musselman left, Emma Rudy and Barbara Herr came to the Mission. They helped in Sunday school, Bible school, and sewing school. Emma Rudy left the mission apartment in 1937 when she became involved in what was then called the "Colored Mission" (later to be

Above: Martha Frederick, Harry Reedel (talking to Joe) Joseph Bromley, and Ted Leslie (son-in-law of Joseph) about 1966.
At right: Mary Bromley, wife of Joseph - 1930

Diamond Street Mennonite Church). Sister Barbara was a very petite, neat, plainly dressed woman who was devoted to the Lord and the people of the neighborhood.

Hettie Kulp - 1900,
married J.D. Minninger

Rules and Conduct for Mennonite dress

Until 1943, Lancaster Conference Mennonites did not have written rules for how they were to dress. In this year, the first "Rules and Discipline" handbook was written which described the proper attire of church members.

The "Brethren" were to wear a regulation, plain coat. They were highly encouraged to omit a tie completely. "Sisters" had greater restrictions. All were to wear plain dresses that were "full enough to cover the form". The bonnets were to be plain, and the coverings, which were worn underneath the bonnet, were not to be round. Jewelry and stylish hairdressing were "unscriptural". Stylish coats, shoes, and stockings were "unbecoming to modesty and meekness of spirit".

17

She brought to church in her car children who lived beyond walking distance. Her apartment was always open to guests and she frequently had church attenders stay for Sunday dinner. She was known to renew her strength daily through personal Bible study and prayer. Earnestine Agnew tells of the mentoring that she received from Sister Barbara. Barbara assisted in the care of Earnestine's mother before her death. She taught Earnestine how to budget her money and other skills needed to live and manage an apartment alone[19].

Fred Yocum also remembers Sister Barbara visiting in his home, assisting his ill mother with household chores and childcare. Fred grew up attending Sunday School and church at Norris Square. After spending time in the U.S. Navy, he returned to Norris Square, committing his life to Christ and the church. His dedication to the Norris Square congregation was strong. In 1952 he married Mary Zimmerman from Bareville. They raised five children in the Mount Airy section of Philadelphia.

Ernestine Agnew with her sister Eleanor

Other sister workers were Mabel (Weaver) Marner, Ruth (Miller) Stauffer, Anna Coulson, and, for a longer time, Katherine Hess. Katherine Hess grew up in the Strasburg Mennonite Church. She was active in the Child Evangelism Movement and was often equipped with various educational materials for children, including a flannelgraph that was used for teaching Bible stories. A very disciplined person, she enjoyed spiritual retreats at places like Keswick, New Jersey. She was known to relate well to her Sunday School teen-age girls and girls' club.

After Barbara Herr retired, Rebecca Frederick, a nurse, moved in with Katherine Hess as a self-supporting worker. When Katherine left in 1956, others, such as Mabel Herr and Anna Mary Keller, shared the apartment with Rebecca.

During the Depression years, 1930 to 1932, the Mission became the distribution center for truckloads of food, two times a week, produced by the Mennonites and Amish of Eastern Pennsylvania. This happened through informal church arrangements, rather than through any formal church relief efforts. As the mission workers wished to provide spiritual nourishment as well as physical nourishment, they required that at least one of the parents should attend one service a week. The sanctuary of the tiny mission was flooded with visitors. Extra preaching services were

Bible School Class - Teacher: Paul Histand, Students: Charlotte (Yocum) Connley, Bernice (Bromley) Rae, Dorothy (Trujeck) Conant, Evelyn (Bromley) Leslie, David Frederick, Fred Yocum.

Front row: Barbara Herr, Mary Rohrer, Katherine Hess, Second row: Rebecca Frederick, Melville Nafziger, Miriam (Miller) Housman, Third row: Aaron King, Jacob Frederick, Fourth row: Elam Kurtz, Clarence Fretz, Roy Kreider.

18

What are you, "A Holy Roller"?

After years of attending the Norris Square services, Yocum finally decided to become a member in 1950. At the time, union membership was forbidden among Lancaster Conference Mennonite churches (a rule that was not normally an issue in the rural churches) and Yocum held a good-paying job at a unionized upholstering factory. Yocum convinced both Pastor Fretz and the union boss to a new agreement that was most certainly unprecedented for both the union and the church. He approached the union boss shortly before his baptism:

Fred and Mary Yocum

"I have something to talk to you about but I don't want you to say anything until I'm finished. It's not going to sound right... I said, I have joined a church, ...and I'm not allowed to belong to a union. Its not a matter of money. The same amount of money that collected for dues I'm willing to give for the charity of the choosing of the union. I will not attend meetings, and for that I will not participate in any of the union benefits, the health, retirement. So I said I would forfeit the benefits of the union and I could not picket. I said, 'that's about it'. He looked right at me and asked, 'What are you a Holy Roller?!'. . I said to him, 'I didn't think you'd understand, so send another man down to the plant'. He said, 'what do you mean?' I said 'I'm leaving' and I headed toward the door. You could see him change. And, you know, he gave me everything I wanted... I got it documented, went back to Clarence (Fretz), and told him. He accepted that, but he said a bishop will come down from Lancaster County to verify the agreement. He never came."

held to provide for the resulting large attendance. Additional volunteer preachers came from both Franconia and Lancaster Conferences. Graybill estimated that between August and September of 1932, approximately 1500 families received some food relief from the mission[20]. This continued until city and state agencies were organized to help the needy.

The early twentieth century witnessed northbound migrations of African-Americans who journeyed to industrial cities, including Philadelphia, looking for economic opportunities that were no longer available in the South as a result of the technological and industrial innovation in farming and manufacturing. Violence and racist social policy often accompanied these population shifts as the former overwhelmingly white city began to experience racial diversification and integration. The small Mennonite mission was not isolated from these changing social dynamics in Philadelphia. Although it is difficult to ascertain from church service attendance records, Good (1995) dates 1934 as the year in which the first African-American families began attending the Mennonite mission on North Howard Street. White Mennonite leaders and members there were unsure how to respond. Racial tension and conflict gripped the city. The "sister workers" began to encounter occasional fights in their Sunday School between white and black children. Initially, everyone worshiped and participated in the Sunday School together regardless of race, but this soon would change. Emma Rudy, a mission worker at the time, recalls that period in her diary:

With the opening of Summer Bible School and Week-day Bible School there came an increased attendance of the colored race to our schools. This was not without its problems, which added to the conviction of opening a work for them...For one WBS (Winter Bible School) term and the following SBS (Summer Bible School) session they were taught in separate schools here at the Mission. Then again for one WBS session (because of a lack of teachers) they were taught in the same school. By this time there was a wider conviction, and deeper than ever, that there should be a work provided for that race[21].

As alluded to by Rudy, it was felt that a separate work should be opened for black people. Despite the fact that the mission had been able to accommodate individuals from European immigrant groups for the first three decades of its existence, racial exclusivity won out when African-Americans wanted to participate. Anna Frederick, a member of the Norris Square church from 1951 to 1970, described the attitudes of white Mennonites at this time as it was told to her:

...black people came to our Sunday school and so on and became members. Part of our congregation at that point said, "what happens when our daughters want to marry them and our sons want to marry their daughters?"...and not long after that, the church decided that it would only be best if a separate mission was set up for black people.

Thus, the fear of racial interaction based on myths of superiority led to the avoidance of the first opportunity for an integrated Mennonite church setting in Philadelphia. On March 10, 1935, only a year after African-Americans began attending the mission, the Mennonite Mission Board approved J. Paul Graybill's "request for opening mission work among the colored folks in the vicinity of the Philadelphia mission; same to be entirely separate from the present mission and in rented quarters"[22]. The new mission for African-Americans was opened at 191 West Dauphin Street a few blocks from the first mission, and later moved to the present site at Diamond Street Mennonite Church. We describe the subsequent history of this congregation in the next section of the book.

In 1939, the Weaverland District, of which Philadelphia was a part, chose a new bishop by lot, a process whereby a number of male nominees were asked to choose from the same number of Bibles set before them. The one who chose the only Bible with a scripture verse written on a piece of paper inside, was considered "chosen" by God. The lot fell on J. Paul Graybill, a culmination , he said , "of many years of premonition".

Graybill, who often wearied of the urban church work[23], had already asked to be relieved of the preaching duties at the Howard Street mission in order to concentrate his efforts on the "colored mission"[24]. The Graybills and their children left Philadelphia and returned to the Weaverland area, though he retained Bishop oversight of the Philadelphia missions until 1965.

The Mission celebrated its fortieth anniversary in 1939. This year was a landmark in the history of the Mission. Steps had been taken to ordain a deacon, and Joseph Bromley, a first-generation Mennonite of the baptismal class of 1927, was chosen. The quarters were enlarged the previous year, and the name changed to Norris Square Mennonite Church in order to signify its transition from mission work to an established congregation. Bromley, a

The Clarence Fretz family
Paul, Lois, Rachel, Clarence and Lela holding Esther

Philadelphia native, had suggested changing the name to Trinity Mennonite Church, but this was quickly vetoed by Graybill who did not consider the name "Mennonite enough". Instead, the name reflected the name of the park that was located across the street from the church buildings. The congregation numbered over forty members and was on a partly self-supporting basis.

When J. Paul Graybill was chosen as Bishop for the Weaverland District and their family left Philadelphia, Clarence Fretz came to pastor the church and be the mission superintendent. Fretz had grown up in Bucks County, Pennsylvania, just north of the city. He was an educated man as was J. Paul Graybill and they shared many of the same concerns for teaching the Word and holding to a strict discipline. He was ordained on June 16, 1940, shortly before he was married on September 15 of that same year to Lela Eshleman, whom he had met during his student years at Eastern Mennonite College.

Clayton and Martha Frederick - 1964

Brother Fretz wrote many articles for church papers such as The Christian Monitor and Gospel Herald. He also wrote reports to his bishop (J. Paul Graybill), perhaps monthly. These writings were in addition to his full schedule of worship services, Sunday School, midweek services, Bible Schools, special meetings and visitation.

Fretz continued the tradition that Graybill had begun of holding firmly to church doctrine and lifestyle. Fred Yocum, who joined the church during Fretz's pastorate, remembers him as a good mentor, but an unyielding disciplinarian: "He took things very, very serious...I've always said that with someone like my pastor...if you even compromise with him, you were better off than a lot of people who went all the way with someone else. But he didn't do much compromising"[25]. Yet, Yocum himself did find a way to generate a compromise from Fretz upon admission to the church (see sidebar on previous page).

During the years of Fretz's pastorate, 1940 to 1951, Jacob W. Frederick, a farmer's son from north of Philadelphia, was ordained to assist in the ministry (1947). For several years there was a leadership team of three ordained persons at Norris Square - Clarence Fretz, resident pastor; Joseph Bromley, deacon; and Jacob Frederick, assistant pastor.

Jacob's parents, Clayton and Martha Frederick, had showed an early interest in the Philadelphia Mennonite Mission. They visited during a snow blizzard while on their honeymoon. A friend of theirs was a member at that time. In 1941, they with their family - a girl and five boys - moved to a farm just north of Philadelphia. They became active members at Norris Square. During the years of gas rationing, they often rode the bus from the city line to the church - an hour or more ride - sometimes twice on Sunday. They were a resource to the church folks for eggs and other farm produce. In addition, many of the city folk would journey to their farm for week-ends to experience life in the country[26].

"Progressive Conservatives"

During the Fretz years, the congregation continued to struggle over the implications of traditional Mennonite cultural symbols, such as dress, that set them apart from the world as they also attempted to reach out to the world in intentional evangelism. Graybill, though no longer living in Philadelphia, continued to keep a close eye on the Philadelphia District so that they did not stray too far from traditional Mennonite practice. Jacob Frederick, assistant pastor in the 1940's remembers these times: "There was a Catholic Church facing our building on the other side of the square. There was a great fear that our ministry in Philadelphia was pro-Catholic. So much so that the pastor, Clarence Fretz, screened all of the pictures that came into our congregation, such as calendars and cards that were given out in Sunday School, so that they didn't have any halos - because that was very Catholic oriented[50]".

One major event in the history of the Philadelphia church that also impacted many Mennonites from the Lancaster area was the development of the Missionary Training Institute, begun in 1947, and lasting for twenty years. Young adults from Mennonite churches throughout southeastern Pennsylvania came to the Institute for intensive training in evangelism. The Institute consisted of an array of speakers with missionary experience,

Missionary Training Institute - 1952 - Front row: Bessie Good, Barbara Herr, John Winters, Henry Garber, J. Irvin Lehman, Jacob Frederick, Anna Frederick, Ada Myer, Second row: Katherine Hess, Rachel Kraybill, Almeda (King) Stoltzfus, – Beiler, – , Mary Miller, Lois (Graybill) Dagen, Lydia (Sensenig) Kurtz, Delores –, Hettie Musser, Third row: Ruth Graybill, Arthur Kraybill, Stephen Stoltzfus, Eugene Beiler, – , Lester Miller, Paul Dagen, Paul Kurtz, – , Miriam Stoltzfus, Fourth row: – , – , Lois Thomas, Martha (Denlinger) Stahl, – , – , Florence Miller, – , Fifth row: Norman Shirk, – Peritoni, Ralph Weaver, Clyde Witmer, – , – , Wilbert Lind, – , Harold Shultz.

as well as practical opportunities to apply their mission skills within the city. In 1947, Henry F. Garber, then President of Eastern Mennonite Missions, wrote in the Missionary Messenger:

> This is a new undertaking for our Board. It is an attempt to provide good counsel and instruction, combined with practical experience, for the young people who have a deep concern for the unsaved. The group will be limited this year because the work is new and our facilities limited. The school will be held at Norris Square Mission in Philadelphia, August 4 - 11 inclusive ... Students who are accepted for the course will receive free lodging and board for the week. Other interested persons are invited to sit in for any of the sessions. All leaders of the discussions are brethren who have experience in their various fields. This week of study and fellowship ought to prove a blessing to our young people and to the cause of missions.

2151 N. Howard (white arch doorway) - Mission Home; one story building is church; three story building to the right is Sunday School building.

TESTMONIES of persons attending Missionary Training Institute

Hackman's Book Store to your Door - At back of Book Store - Mary Elizabeth (Lutz) Good, Lois (Kraybill) Stahl, Nelson Kauffman, Alma Ruth - 1948

Miriam R. (Weaver) Stoltzfus - 1947

I was among those who came to MTI in its first year. I was invited - I think it was by invitation only. The afternoons of practical work were special - visiting in a hospital ward with Alma Ruth and doing door-to-door canvassing in Oxford Village. This experience made it comfortable to come to live in Philadelphia about 4 years later.

Mary (Harnish) Hess - 1948

This exposure to sharing the gospel in the city was very helpful to me. I had just completed nurses' training and was soon to enter an internship in West Virginia. Living together, students and teachers, for a week at the mission introduced us to the give and take in most mission situations. Classes in Bible and personal witness were helpful. Nelson Kauffman cautioned that one cannot witness to everyone he meets but to be alert to the nudges of the Holy Spirit. Emma Rudy, long time worker in Philadelphia, invit-

ed me to visit with her in several homes in the community. I learned how God uses quiet persons to help others, too.

Mary Elizabeth (Lutz) Good - 1948

Our mornings were spent in Bible study and listening to Biblical messages and learning practical hints about methods of evangelism. Then in the afternoons and evenings we had many opportunities to witness - religious surveys, home visitation, literature

distribution, street meeting, children's open-air classes, going to rest homes, working in the church office, rescue mission services, cottage meetings, and going alone in personal witnessing. I felt so keenly my dependence on the Holy Spirit's leading and His power in these contacts with city strangers.

Luke and Ruth Horst - 1951

We remember the instruction from Bible teachers like J. Irvin Lehman, Milton Brackbill,

Throughout the 1940's, the Mennonites of Philadelphia continued to struggle with the traditional symbols of the church that so separated them from their neighbors in the city. Graybill, although no longer living in the city, still kept his hand in these matters, guiding the dress-code decisions back to tradition whenever possible as evidenced by the following letter he wrote in 1948:

At a meeting today the Norris Square ministry, J. Paul Graybill, Clarence Fretz, Jacob Frederick, and Joseph Bromley we agreed that we would require the following points of the discipline to be adhered to: 1. A square covering with ribbons, 2. A bonnet of discipline size, 3. Dark stockings, 4. Hair combed with part in the middle, 5. No long necktie. These points to apply in daily life.

Agreed that I should explain these matters at a members meeting Jan. 2, 1949 and then deal with those who do not respond after another ministry meeting some time after the above announcement.

- J. Paul Graybill

The Clarence Fretz family left Philadelphia in September of 1951 for an assignment with Eastern Mennonite Missions as missionaries to Luxemburg. There was no Mission Superintendent until Wilmer and Ruth Hollinger came in 1953. At the young age of 19 years old and one month after their wedding, the Hollingers arrived in Philadelphia, unaware of the impact that such an experience would have on their lives. Looking back on this time, they recall:

We had to learn how to live together, how to live in the city, and to discover what we were supposed to be doing. We were to witness, but what did that mean? There was no job description, and hence no sense of accomplishment. There was always more to do than could be done. We could have profited from some cross-cultural training. Dressed in Mennonite garb of the 1950's - caped dress, black stockings,

Missionary Training Institute - Front row are staff: Wilmer Hollinger, Paul Kraybill, Milton Brackbill, James Shank, Luke Stoltzfus, John Winters, Marie Keener, – , Dorothy Heller, – , Grace Witmer, Huldah Graybill, Rachel (Landis) Stahl, Mrs. Paul Martin, – , Connie Stauffer, Mrs. Wilbur Leaman, Jacob Stahl, Paul Martin, – , Harold Stauffer, Wilbur Leaman, – , – , Lloyd Wenger, David Shenk, Ray Witmer, – Herbert Heller, Ruth Burkholder, Helen (Longenecker) Lapp, – Burkholder - 1958.

Paul and Lydia S. Kurtz - 1952

I enjoy hearing about men being used of God, but to see men of God at work before my eyes challenged me. Seeing our instructors and our activity leaders meet situations successfully was inspiring. Other young folks, devoted to God, caused me to see the power of God. Most of all, I enjoyed the guidance and blessing of God personally. I will often be refreshed in my Christian experience by remembering the valuable training of the Institute.

Harold S. Stauffer - 1958

Our instructors included men like David Thomas, Noah Hershey, James Shank, Paul N. Kraybill, Ira J. Buckwalter, John Winters, and Luke Stoltzfus. We were challenged to present the pure gospel with as little of our own "cultural flavor" as possible, allowing the individual believer to discover what applications the Spirit would lead him to make.

Raymond Charles, and others. We were sent out alone on the streets of Philadelphia to witness to whomever we could find. Ruth witnessed to a Jewish girl and realized that she needed more ready Scripture at her command. We remember that the men and women slept in separate dormitories and enjoyed the good conversations we had with each other. We came home with the determination to be better witnesses for Christ.

Wilmer and Ruth Hollinger family - Ruth holding Judy, Lynda and Wilmer - 1958

and covering - set Ruth apart the minute she stepped out the front door. We learned by experience what it meant to trust God[27].

Sundays were working days for Wilmer, beginning with the bringing of several car loads of children to Sunday School and ending with taking a cerebral palsy member to his home on the outskirts of the city. On Communion Sundays, all of the members stayed for dinner. The sister workers prepared the meal and then hurried into church for the afternoon communion service. Communion Sundays also brought the Bishop from Lancaster County to the city to read the Statement of Rules and Discipline to the congregation. Wilmer remembers one mischievous Sunday School boy who, after listening to all of the Bishop's rules, leaned over to his teacher and asked, "Who does all that?".

During the early 1950's, Jacob Frederick was enrolled at Eastern Mennonite College in preparation to become the lead pastor when he returned to Philadelphia after his marriage to Anna Horst, a Registered Nurse from Maryland, in 1951. Jacob's installment as lead pastor at Norris Square in that same year was the beginning of more than two decades of leadership provided by the Frederick family at the Norris Square and Oxford Circle congregations.

Jacob and Anna Frederick moved into the mission home at 2151 North Howard Street in 1951. Jacob's parents, Clayton and Martha, bought a home in the next block and became more involved in the daily activities and witnessing for years to come. Jacob and Anna served more than twenty years and raised six children in Philadelphia.

The Norris Square Mennonite Church continued to acquire a diverse array of individuals, some of whom came from Mennonite background and others who did

Art McPhee: The making of a Mennonite sailor
- written by Linford Martin

After teaching a Sunday School class, I went downstairs to the worship service. The congregation at Norris Square was small, so

Art McPhee as a sailor - 1967

it was easy to spot a young sailor dressed in full Navy uniform. My first thought was that he must be lost, that he was in the wrong church for a military man. After all, we were conscientious objectors.

I was curious about him, but I didn't know if I wanted to talk with him because I had been in so many debates defending my position as a conscientious objector to military service. While the preacher was talking to him after church, I finally got around to visiting with him. Jacob suggested that Donnie and I take this sailor, Art McPhee, home with us for lunch.

It turned out that Art was a very interesting young man. He had become a believer from his own study of the Bible, had read about Mennonites, and was interested in learning more. He was the easiest person I have ever witnessed to; he was full of questions and was so inspiring to be around. He stayed all afternoon, ate supper with us, and went to church again on Sunday night. That was the beginning of a relationship with members of our household. He continued coming every Sunday that his ship was in port in Philadelphia, until he got out of the Navy.

Art later turned down a full scholarship at the Naval Academy in Annapolis to go to Eastern Mennonite College.

Despite his lack of knowledge of Mennonites at first arrival at the Norris Square Church, Art McPhee, a well-known writer, now is a professor at the Associated Mennonite Biblical Seminary in Elkhart, Indiana.

not. Henry Mack moved from Spring City and operated a grocery store in North Philadelphia. He was a good song leader and taught the women's Sunday School class. He served on the Wednesday evening program committee and visited older men in their homes. Mack would often time the length of the service. If it went past the usual closing time, he would stomp his foot on the floor loud enough for the pastor to hear. Rose Kaiser was a German woman who lived with her daughter and son-in-law (Ed Kessler) about two blocks from the church. She learned to read English by reading the Bible. She often said, "I don't pray for myself; I pray for others." Emma Showalter was a lab technician who worked at Temple University Hospital. She taught and supported Norris Square about fifteen years. Her home was a place of refreshment for other single Mennonite ladies working in the city.

Jacob and Anna Frederick Family - front row: Naomi, Jacob, Anna, Philip, Jacob, Carl, Ray, Mariann - 1972

In 1961, Giday Belete, the wife of Million Belete, was baptized by Bishop J. Paul Graybill at Norris Square. The Belete family was from Ethiopia where it was illegal at the time to perform Christian baptisms. They were in Philadelphia while Million continued his education under an Ethiopian government scholarship. The two would later become leaders in the Meserete Kristos Church in Ethiopia and Million would eventually complete a term as President of the Mennonite World Conference.

Henry Mack - 1940

Dr. Merle and Sara Eshelman - 1940

Many medical students and others helped with various programs over the years. Dr. Merle and Sarah Eshelman lived in two rooms at 2151 North Howard Street with Merle's sister and brother-in-law, Clarence and Lela Fretz. Although the attendance of medical students brought much-needed human resources to the church work, their bent toward modernity often led to some conflict with the more traditional church leaders. A 1960 meeting of Philadelphia Mennonite church leaders noted this dilemma: "The problem of Mennonite students taking communion and supporting the work in our mission churches with long ties, no capes, taking off coverings immediately following the service, was discussed with concern by all. The influence left is very destructive and breaks down convictions which we seek to build"[28]. A few years later, a gathering of the Mennonite Students Fellowship in Philadelphia prompted even more controversy when participants acted out a play that included violence and recited a poem about a drunken man[29].

Other missionary candidates who helped during their time in Philadelphia were John and Catharine Leatherman (1935-36), Noah and Muriel Mack (1936-38), Daniel and Blanche Sensenig (1944), and Richard and Gail Kling (1947-48). Dr. Vernon Kratz, who lived with Clayton and Martha Frederick, was considered an asset and role model to the church while he attended medical school during the 1960s.

From 1960 to 1972 Philadelphia had a program known as "Model Cities" to curb blight in older sections of the city. Jacob Frederick received a plaque from "Model Cities" - "Recognizing unselfish service to the community". This was recognition of the intense community efforts that the church put into addressing the social needs of their surrounding neighborhood during this time period. The Norris Square congregation did not act alone, and community involvement included working with the ministerium of neighboring churches to address the social problems that they identified in the community. This collaboration led to a reduction in the number of saloons in the area as local pastors would speak out against drinking establishments. A children's playground was built. College scholarships were given for needy students; and the Frederick family was actively involved with the local Parent-Teacher Association. Anna worked as School Nurse in the area. The Frederick family rehabilitated a house at 1916 Hancock Street that had been unoccupied for several years, and moved into it. It inspired others to paint and repair. Twenty-five years later this is still a nice block of homes.

One of the most noted programs run by the Norris Square Mennonite Church was "Operation Hayseed", a summertime program in which Lancaster County Churches could host a busload of children and parents for a day in the country. One host family, Mervin and Edith Weiler, wrote of this experience:

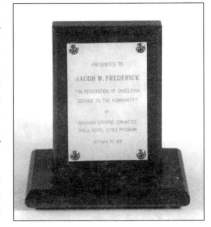

Plaque for Model Cities - 1971

"We always looked forward to having the group from Philadelphia come to the farm for a visit. It was a special day for all of us. Our church family would come, too, to help and to enjoy the day. Things like this bring us closer together. We looked forward to seeing the joy on the faces of the children as they got off the bus. When evening came, some did not want to go back to the city. This would tug at our heart strings. We wished we could accommodate them longer. Its something we will never forget!"

Through the late 1960's and into the early 70's, the population of the surrounding Kensington community began to change dramatically. A neighborhood that used to consist primarily of European immigrant working class families, began to see more African-American and Hispanic families begin to move into the neighborhood. As these changes occurred, the church began to invite Spanish-speaking families to their services and events, some of whom accepted and began to be incorporated into the congregation despite the fact that many were limited in their English. By 1970, a separate afternoon service held in Spanish was initiated by Jose Santiago and Eugenio Matos. Jose Santiago, who had been pastoring a New Holland Mennonite church often preached at these services. George Miller, a Mennonite consultant who had spent time in Central America, was asked to help with the cultural and linguistic differences that existed between the congregational old-timers and the Hispanic newcomers.

Wagon rides at the Weiler Farm - 1971

Bus at the Beidler Farm - At left: Martha Frederick, at right: Anna Frederick, couple at the bus is Galen and Janice Martin

In order to fill an empty pastoral position at the Oxford Circle Mennonite Church in Philadelphia, Jacob Frederick left Norris Square in 1970 after twenty years as lead pastor. He was replaced by Jim Leaman, who had earlier assisted Jacob. Jim and his wife Beth had come to Philadelphia in 1969 as voluntary service workers in order for Jim to fulfill his service requirements as a conscientious objector. With counsel from the EMM voluntary service Director Leon Stauffer, he had initiated a youth ministry related to the Norris Square congregation, gathering youth from a variety of racial backgrounds together to shoot pool in a renovated basement recreation room, shoot baskets on the outside courts, or camp in areas outside of the city. About three-fourths of the way through his two-year assignment, Jim was licensed as a minister to assist Frederick at the Norris Square congregation. Pastor Jacob introduced him to the local ministerium. Today, he reflects that his "horizons of the Christian community were broadened widely from my Mennonite upbringing and my eyes were opened to social justice concerns"[30].

In 1974, the Norris Square membership, which by now was primarily only a few elderly individuals, disbanded and joined other Mennonite churches in the city. Some went to Oxford Circle. Some went to Frazer Mennonite church in the suburbs. Mary Crawford went to Calvary Holiness on North 2nd Street. Her daughter, Christine (Crawford) Wenger is now a member at New Mercies Mennonite in East Falls.

Ernestine Agnew with Mary Crawford

Arca de Salvacíon Iglesia Evangelica Mennonita

The buildings and the witness of Norris Square became the responsibility of the Spanish congregation which had named itself Arca de Salvacion. By this time, the community had changed to mostly Spanish-speaking residents. The congregation had a Spanish-speaking pastor and was a part of the Delaware Valley District. When a Spanish District was formed by the Conference, they became a part of that. One of the first pastors was Eugenio Matos, who served about two years. He now pastors in Trenton, New Jersey. Benjamin Perez and Isadoro Saez each stayed a couple years. When Saez moved, Arcadio and Matilda Tolentino were licensed to lead the church. Matilda had accepted Christ in evangelistic meetings in 1972, and Arcadio came to Christ through the Bible school. Luke Soltzfus ordained him in 1977. They served the church for twenty years, building the congregation from the eleven when he began to 130 at its peak. When the Tolentinos left the church in 1996, a number of the members also left and the present congregation consists of about twenty-five members. Diodoro Baez and Juan Carmona, the current pastor, have both provided leadership in the congregation's pulpit.

Arca de Salvacion - Eugenio Matos, Angel Sanchez, and José Santiago

Matilda and Arcadio Tolentino - 1999

Discipline and forgiveness
- struggles over identity and tradition

The growth of the Mennonite Church in Philadelphia was not without its struggles. Adherence to authority, tradition, and rules were sticking points that often kept people from joining the church and, at times, forced people out of the church. Two cases of discipline in two Philadelphia congregations illustrate this point.

Norris Square - *Joseph and Mary Bromley had eight children. Joseph was the Deacon of Norris Square Mennonite Church from 1939 to 1957. His entire family, including Joseph's father, was actively involved in the church. Joseph acted as Sunday School teacher and Bible Study leader, as well as Deacon for a number of years. In 1957, it came to the attention of J. Paul Graybill, the District Bishop, that one of the Bromley boys had a television set in his room on the second floor of the house. The bishop asked the deacon to convince his son to remove the TV from the home. When this did not happen, Joseph was "set back from communion" (ex-communicated). As a result, the entire Bromley family resigned their membership in the church and never returned. In later years though, Joseph Bromley was reinstated and received communion while in a retirement home.*

Diamond Street - *The year was 1954. Easter Jackson, mother of Mattie Cooper and Raymond and William Jackson, had earlier terminated her personal relationship with the father of Raymond and William. A neighbor who was also a church member reported that the boys' father was stopping by on a weekly basis. She implied that there were "unholy relationships" continuing. With Bishop Graybill's advice, Pastor Luke and Miriam Stoltzfus visited Easter, asking her to stop these visits from the boy's father. Although she made the plea that she wanted her boys to know their father, since many children in the area grew up not knowing their fathers, her explanation was not accepted and she was ex-communicated. She accepted this decision graciously saying, "That is the rule of the church, so I must yield". However she strongly encouraged her children to stay with the church while she found another denomination. Raymond, her son, eventually became pastor at Diamond Street Mennonite Church and is currently Assistant Pastor at Christian Life Mennonite Church. Mattie, her daughter, today continues to be a primary leader. Forty years later, daughter Mattie urged then Bishop Luke Stoltzfus to offer an apology for the act. The apology was once again graciously received and she assured them that there were no hard feelings. The interesting sequel to this story is that twenty years later, the father became a member at Diamond Street and remained so until his death.*

Diamond Street Mennonite Church

In September of 1926, Emma Rudy began working at the Philadelphia mission with Paul and Phebe Graybill. In the beginning, she was uncertain that the Lord had led her to the right place, but, after a time, she felt at home and enjoyed the work, especially the Bible School that Graybill had begun. In 1930 her health failed and she was unable to work. She had tuberculosis and was advised to leave the city. She recalled the scripture in James 5 and asked to be anointed by the leaders of the church. She eventually recovered and soon resumed her full responsibilities, not knowing at the time that within a few years she would be the sole full-time worker at a new mission at Philadelphia.

In 1934 a few African-American families began attending the Mennonite Mission at 2151 North Howard Street. The Mennonites there were unsure how to respond. Racial tension and conflict gripped the city. Even the little mission had occasional scuffles in their Sunday School. At first white and black children worshipped together. But because of "various problems" that arose it was felt that a separate work should be opened for the African American children. We described this transition more fully in the previous section.

Separate Bible Schools were held for blacks and whites during 1934 and 1935. In March, 1935, EMM approved J. Paul Graybill's "request for opening mission work among the colored folks in the vicinity of the Philadelphia Mission; same to be entirely separate from the present mission and in rented quarters". The Mennonite Mission for the Colored opened at 191 West Dauphin Street a few blocks from the first mission. Here Bible School and Sunday evening services were held for seven years as a sub-church of the original mission.

Emma Rudy took considerable leadership in this new mission and provided stability. Alma Ruth served occasionally from 1936 to 1939, after which she joined Rudy as a full-time missionary. As in the case of the previous Norris Square mission, it was the sister workers who provided the stabilizing presence and leadership for the burgeoning new mission. The preaching was begun by J. Paul Graybill from the "mother" church. Merle Eshelman and Noah K. Mack helped with preaching until they left for missionary service in Africa. G. Irvin Lehman and Clarence Fretz also filled the pulpit for a time.

For the first few years, the "colored" mission, as it was called at the time, was attended primarily by white Mennonites. A few children would occasionally attend the Sunday School and even more came to the Bible School that opened in October 1935. After the first year, Summer Bible School enrollment was between seventy and eighty students with actual attendance varying from a low of twenty-six to a high of ninety-four. Winter Bible School also gained in popularity so that in 1939 registration rivaled the summer school. When adults from the community did attend, the church workers rejoiced, as Emma Rudy did when she wrote, "This evening an outstanding event occurred. For the first time since the work opened, adult folks were present"[31]. One week later though, at the opening of the Bible School, she expressed discouragement in the par-

Emma Rudy, Olivia Smith, Alma Ruth, Pearl Smith - 1954

Emma Rudy and Alma Ruth-Mothers of Diamond Street Mennonite Church

Emma Rudy and Alma Ruth served at Diamond Street for almost twenty years. They were the "pillars" and "founding mothers" of the church. The sister workers provided a stable presence as pastors and Sunday School superintendents would come and go.

In the summer months, Emma and Alma held many "open-air" Bible schools. A vacant lot was often the location. Milk crates with boards across provided seating. An easel with a flannelgraph board and pictures provided the "stage" for Bible stories to come alive.

Charles Baynard once remarked that the sister workers, "... challenged us all by loving us into the fellowship".

Open air Bible School - Person in foreground unknown, teacher in back is Mary Ella Martin

ticipation: "This evening, the Week Day Bible School was opened for colored children and parents. Some visitation had been done and cards were sent to most of the families. The results were not very encouraging as only three colored folks (adults) were present"[32]. Slowly, the sister workers continued to canvass the neighborhoods and visit families, but attendance at the mission was not very consistent. By 1936, one African-American adult male began to attend regularly and five more in 1937. In 1939, this number increased to sixteen[33].

In 1936, Charles Mills became the first African-American in Philadelphia to begin instruction classes for membership into the Mennonite denomination, although he died unexpectedly before he officially became a member. The sister workers tried to maintain a steadfast faith in the work despite poor attendance at meetings: "The colored mission at 191 West Dauphin Street has now been conducted for two years by the Mennonite Church. During this time the work has shown some progress, but so far there are no members of the church at this place. At first the attendance was largely children, but a few adults have come to the meetings. At times, there have been four or five adults present"[34]. On November 27, 1938, the church workers received a boost in their spirits. Alleanor Jenkins and her two daughters Grace and Edna were "received as the first members by the right hand of fellowship"[35].

Alleanor Jenkins with Eric, Dirck and Don Stoltzfus

Despite the short terms of teachers and leadership, the work grew steadily, particularly among children and youth, and soon outgrew its small meeting room. At times, the sisters were trying to pack up to 90 children into the 13 by 26 foot room. The Mission briefly relocated to an empty store at Dauphin and Amber Streets as the Bible School classes for children became larger. Out of hopes for the potential growth of the Mission, EMM authorized a search for the purchase of a suitable property. None was found until 1941, when 1814 West Diamond Street was discovered - a political club that was unoccupied for a number of years. Jacob Hershey from Lancaster and Claude Myers of Franconia coordinated volunteers in renovating the building, making a meeting room on first floor, with apartments for workers on the second and third floors.

Relocation

In 1942, the building was ready for the sister workers, Emma Rudy and Alma Ruth, to occupy. Clinton and Maybelle Ferster were the first resident pastor couple. They stayed two years until they were able to travel to their appointed mission field in Africa that had been delayed by the advent of World War II. This new location of the mission was about twenty blocks from the first and so it was like starting over for the sister workers as they attempted to establish relationships in their new neighborhood. In order to reach out to other parts of the neighborhood, the sister workers would often set up boards and milk crates in empty lots in other blocks, encouraging the children to say the verses so loudly that the neighbors would hear them. The program at the Diamond Street building continued with many of the same elements as at Dauphin Street - Summer and Winter Bible School, visitation, home Bible studies and adding Sunday School and worship services and mid-week ser-

Clinton and Maybelle Ferster - 1942

Above: J. Harold and Margaret Brenneman - 1947, At right: The "Come to Jesus" Church, Pastor Homer Schrock in foreground - 1967

vices. When the Fersters left in 1944, Ezra Nafziger, a medical student, served as superintendent for one year. The next year Clair Bomberger assumed responsibility to obtain preachers for Sundays. James Lark, then pastor at Rocky Ridge Mennonite Church outside of Philadelphia, and his wife Rowena frequently came to the city to assist in the work.

In June of 1946, the sister workers heartily welcomed the coming of J. Harold and Margaret Breneman as the new superintendent couple. Harold was ordained as the first pastor for Diamond Street. They felt called to mission work, but were unfamiliar with large cities and the "difficult life" there. He served as pastor until late 1950. There was significant growth during these years with Summer Bible School attendance at ninety-six. Also, three new persons were baptized as members: Marie Ballard, seventy, and Doris Allen, eleven, and a young mother, Mrs. Murray.

Frank and Katie Garman, who replaced the Brenemans, stayed only five months because Mrs. Garman's health became such that she could not go up stairs. So once again the leadership of the mission floundered in an uncertain future. During these early years a neon sign was erected on the front of 1814 West Diamond Street with an invitation: "Come to Jesus". Thus the mission became known in the community as the "Come to Jesus church". This sign remains in place today outside the daycare center that now occupies the building, but the neon lights have long since been stripped away.

August 29, 1951, was the beginning of a new era for the Diamond Street Mission when Luke and Miriam Stoltzfus moved into the second floor apartment. Fresh from studies at Eastern Mennonite College, Luke was to be the new pastor at the Mission. Emma Rudy and Alma Ruth had kept the mission functioning consistently and

Luke and Miriam Stoltzfus Family
Miriam (holding Glenn) Rhoda and Luke

Mattie (Cooper) Nikiema

A Graduate from Nursing School - 1960

When I was almost fourteen we moved to another neighborhood, still located in what we now call "the ghetto". During this time my mother was quite ill and we struggled to make ends meet. At this time two very simply, but oddly attired white ladies came to our apartment door and invited us to their church nearby. They wore the white prayer caps and extremely simply made dresses and black footwear. They said they were Mennonites. We had never heard of these people before, and white folks didn't invite us to accompany them anywhere. You can imagine our perplexity on the appearance of these "sisters". Finally after many invitations and an admonition "not to dress up", we began to attend worship services at this small interracial Mennonite Church. We responded eagerly to the warm welcome extended by this group and to the "gospel of love and equality", evidenced by this community of believers. We quickly formed alliances with other blacks in the area who were a part of this "Come to Jesus Church" as it was called by the children, alluding to a large neon cross on the front bearing those words.

As a Mennonite girl, my main conflict was between the distinctive dress and my peer group. While going to school, I didn't wear the uniform dress, only the prayer cap. Even so, that was enough to separate me from my peers and induce lots of questions on their part. My peers and other blacks were usually unfamiliar with my beliefs. My teachers and other whites were often acquainted with Mennonites but only thought of them as honest, hardworking people of Dutch descent and good cooks; so, I became quite fluent in informing them of the proselytizing, evangelical nature of the Mennonites. It is still amusing to see the reaction of some whites when confronted by a black Mennonite.

*This is an excerpt of a paper that Mattie wrote for a sociology class in 1973.

now the Stoltzfuses were determined, like the two women, to stay in Philadelphia. They made Philadelphia their home - a place to raise their six children and to actively serve the Mennonite Church.   Church members later commented on their gratefulness for the openness of the Stoltzfus home: "Luke and Miriam will never know what it meant that we could go to their home when we wished"[36]. Henry Garber, chairman of EMM, had asked the Stoltzfuses to come to Diamond Street and he told them, "The sister workers have been there a long time and they will have much to offer you - but remember that you are the leaders". As a young man in a new role, Stoltzfus nonetheless often turned to the wisdom and experience of Rudy and Ruth. Later he remarked that he "received his pastoral internship training from the two sister workers[37]", a rare occurrence in the male-dominated church of that time.

A Time for Change

When Stoltzfus came in 1951, the mission's checkbook read "African Mennonite Mission", a name that had been suggested by James Lark. He promptly changed it to read "Diamond Street Mennonite Church" in the hopes of establishing the mission as a more permanent congregation. At the time, there were only three members and average Sunday morning attendance was about twenty-five. In the following years, attendance and membership

Summer Bible School - 1952 (5th grade – Adult) Third row fourth person - Algie DeWitt, fourth row second person - Margie Fields, eleventh person - Barbara (Allen) Baynard, Teacher Rhoda (Stoltzfus) Glick, fifth row - Teacher Alvie Beachy, seventh girl is Margaret Allen, twelth girl is Emily DeWitt., sixth row - Teachers Ralph Shank and Harry Lefever. To the right Teachers Emma Rudy, Alma Ruth, Helen Fry and Sister Rowena Lark, last row third girl Doris (Allen) Perkins, last boy is Henry Lucas.

rose steadily. Summer and Winter Bible School for children were the most popular of the Church's programs.

Marie Ballard was one of the three members at Diamond Street in 1951. She lived on Woodstock Street a few blocks from the church. In the years prior to the Stoltzfus' arrival, Sisters Emma Rudy and Alma Ruth visited her and gave her instruction in the Bible and in the rules and discipline of the Mennonite Church. When she neared the decision of membership, she felt unsure of whether she should join this group who seemed so different to her. She was elderly and unable to read and check the truth of what she was being taught by these two sisters. In earnest quest for what was truth, she knelt by her bed in prayer. While kneeling there, she experienced a wrap around her shoulders, warm and comforting. She understood this as God's sign that the sisters were speaking the truth and that she could trust them and the church they represented.

During the 1950's, camping and various types of "Fresh Air" programs were begun. The first camp used was Menn-o-lan in Quakertown and then Tel Hai in Honeybrook, until Camp Hebron, a retreat north of Harrisburg, was opened. The Fresh Air program gave city children a week or two with a Mennonite family in the country. Many long-term relationships developed lasting into adulthood.

Another concern that the church addressed was the need for care and security for elderly members. In 1954, Bethany Mennonite Home was established in order to care for the aging members at the Diamond Street congregation. Homer Schrock wrote that Bethany Mennonite Home "became a home with a Christian atmosphere for eleven guests: seven ladies and four men"[38]. Bethany also became a guesthouse for Lancaster County Mennonites who came to serve at Bethany. It was located a block from the church (1910 West Diamond Street) which gave both staff and guests a spiritual base. Bethany was owned and operated by EMM. Several of the elderly guests accepted Christ for the first time, one even after age eighty-five. Guests often felt abandoned by their kin. In those times the staff became their loving and caring family. One resident, Sister Ballard, had a lively sense of humor. Shaking her cane at the staff was never a threat, but her way of relating with the staff.

Mary Horning (Mahoney), Esther Stover, Esther Kurtz (Mann), Grace Hess, and Mattie Nikiema and a host of other faithful volunteers gave the day-to-day care. The Home was always managed by a superintendent and matron couple. These included Stephen and Almeda Stoltzfus and Jason and Miriam Stoltzfus. In 1957, Homer and Ruth Schrock came to work at Bethany. Others who served in this capacity were Calvin and Lily Beiler, Sam and Helen Haldeman, Tom and Vernie Miller, and Christ and Ruth Breneman. For various reasons, increasing state regulations and diminishing need, the home closed for care of the elderly and reopened later as Bethany Child Care Center ministering to preschool children.

Marie Ballard and Mary Moyer at Bethany Home - 1961

The Homer and Ruth Schrock Family Homer, Linda, Orpha, and Ruth Schrock

The Calvin and Lily Beiler Family Calvin, Keith, Valerie, Dwilyn, and Lily

Of covering strings and tradition

Women in the Mennonite Church during the 1950's were expected to wear a covering on their head and Lancaster Conference standards also dictated that the coverings have long strings attached on the side. One day, Pastor Luke Stoltzfus overheard a young Philadelphia girl who was considering membership at Diamond Street to say, "I can't wait until I get to wear those pretty strings on my covering!". It didn't take long for Stoltzfus to realize that the intended meaning for the covering and strings, that of separation from the world, had somehow become a worldly fashion statement. The young girl never got to wear her strings.

In the early 1960s Charles Baynard and his sister Florence (Baynard) Grimes, originally from the Andrew's Bridge Mennonite Church, began attending Diamond Street. Charles met Barbara Allen and they were married in 1961. Charles and Barbara provided stability for the congregation as lay members for a number of years until Charles joined the pastoral team in the 1970's. Florence and her four children, Beatrice (Macon), Barbara (Bell), Asa, Jr. and Daniel became pillars as well. Father Asa joined the other family members after the children were grown.

In October 1961, Emma Rudy and Alma Ruth left the apartment they had occupied since 1942 and moved to a home for retired missionaries in Lancaster County. Mattie Cooper Nikiema

Church group at Andrew's Bridge, Lancaster County - Back row: Asa Grimes, Florence (Baynard) Grimes, Myrtle and Walter Baynard, Charles C. Baynard, first row: woman not known, 3 children of Walter Baynard, Florence Beatrice (Bea) Baynard (Mother of Florence) and Charles.

Asa and Florence (Baynard) Grimes with daughter Beatrice

The Macon Family - Michael, Joseph, Gunsala, Beatrice (Grimes), Corinne, Katrina Macon

remembers them fondly: "Their work of visitation was very important because as women they had access to the many single parent families that no man could have or would have chosen to enter"[39]. After decades of intense commitment to evangelism work in the Philadelphia area, Rudy and Ruth returned to the countryside. They are still remembered today by many who were nurtured by them.

By 1965 attendance at Sunday services reached an average of one hundred and membership around forty. Among those attending were six siblings of Doris Allen (Perkins)- Margaret, Barbara (Baynard), Clarence, Thomas, James, and Isaac. Easter Jackson and her children, Mattie Cooper (Nikiema), and Raymond and William Jackson were also members. The Allen and Jackson families have both played an active role in the church through the years.

The Turbulent 60's

During the summers of 1964 and 1965, fierce riots erupted throughout the city of Philadelphia. The nation was nearing the peak of a long struggle for equal opportunity and racial justice. The leaders of the Civil Rights movement had succeeded in bringing about increased attention to the plight of black America and to the horrendous discrimination and racism that African Americans faced in their daily lives. This threatened the historical legacy of white dominance in the U.S. Police cars with lights flashing and sirens blaring raced back and forth on Diamond Street. Those days were reminiscent of the disturbances on Howard Street in 1910 where, during the strike of the Philadelphia Transit Company workers, nearly 300 streetcars were wrecked and 3000 windows smashed. Just to be on the street was dangerous in those violent weeks, but no harm was ever done to the Diamond Street Mennonite building. Pastor Luke and Miriam Stoltzfus continued going about their daily activities providing a stable presence within the church. Members such as Raymond Jackson, Charles Baynard, and their families continued their active role in the community and challenged the congregation to continue to incorporate the broader social justice struggles with their evangelistic work.

By now, Lancaster Conference officials had determined that the Philadelphia churches were growing fast enough and held enough potential that a separate district was to be established for them. In January 1965, Luke Stoltzfus was chosen by lot from a group of four area ministers (including Stoltzfus, Jacob Frederick, Roy Newswanger, and Clarence Fretz) to be the Bishop of the Philadelphia-Chester District. The lot process involved the four pastors each choosing from four Bibles on a table prepared for the ceremony. The one who chose the Bible with a scripture verse from Proverbs written on a piece of paper within, was considered "chosen" by God to be the Bishop.

Stoltzfus' change in role brought many changes to the life and practice of Philadelphia Mennonites. A first consideration was a new pastor for Diamond Street. Homer Schrock was chosen by congregational vote, the first pastor to be called from within the congregation. Since older male members were rare at the time and he was the only person nominated, the process of choosing by the lot was not necessary. He was ordained in May 1965. He and Ruth

34

were regular and active members since they came to the city to be at Bethany Home. When the Stoltzfus family moved from the Diamond Street church building to West Philadelphia in June 1967, the Schrocks chose to stay in their home at 1908 Fontain Street (about one block away) rather than move into the church apartment. The pastor living "among" his members was a departure from the "mission outlook". The Stoltzfus era of sixteen years (1951- 1965) shaped the little mission into a church recognized by the Lancaster Conference. A nucleus of members of a more autonomous church would continue the vision.

The Allen Family

Thomas, Issac, James, Clarence, Estelle, Doris (Allen) Perkins, Barbara (Allen) Baynard, Margaret

Residents of the immediate community, the Allen family were the single largest family involved at Diamond Street Mennonite church. Doris and Margaret became members around 1950. Barbara, Clarence, Thomas, Jimmy, and Isaac followed over the next few years. Clarence was an outgoing and aggressive person who was often in demand by churches for his gifts as a chorister. The Allen family provided a stable presence in the congregation during the turbulent period of the 60's and 70's.

The Luke and Miriam Stoltzfus Family - front row: Eric, Luke, Miriam, Theda, Don, Glenn, Rhoda, Dirck - 1968

Sewing Circle at DSMC - Barbara (Allen) Baynard, Eula Greene, Mattie (Cooper) Nikiema, Ruth (Petersheim) Schrock, Miriam (Weaver) Stoltzfus

Schrock asked for a church cabinet to aid him in decision-making. This was a new development in the structure of the church that assisted in the breaking down of the hierarchical structure. Boys club and Girls club were initiated, integrating Bible Study with craft projects. There was Sewing Circle for the women, as well as a community ministry known as "Home Builders", sending Christian literature to families at important times in life, like births, marriages, and deaths.

In the spring of 1970, the congregation decided to call an assistant pastor. Raymond Jackson, twenty-five years old, born and raised in North Philadelphia, was the man. He and six volunteers launched a summer day camp called "Adventures in Brotherhood", with ambitious goals of changing lives and saving souls. For five days a week, the camp offered children opportunities in education, Bible study, camping, creativity and service. The summer was highly successful as a result of the day camp being so popular.

When Schrock left at the end of 1970 to further his education in Grantsville, Maryland, Raymond Jackson was chosen by congregational vote to become the lead pastor. Charles Baynard was licensed as his assistant. The vote heralded a new era in the history of the Lancaster Conference Philadelphia churches. For the first time, a person of color was given the lead pastoral role. During the next four years, the congregation would begin to plant the seeds for the tremendous growth that was to follow in the late 1970's.

Jackson brought a progressive vision of community outreach and theological groundedness that inspired the congregation to begin to think in creative new ways about the future of the church. Initially, this was somewhat troubling to a few of the older members of the congregation who considered this young man whom they had known as a child to be departing too rapidly from the old Mennonite ways. The turmoil of the 1960's had spilled over into the 1970's and cries for black liberation continued to spill out into the streets of Philadelphia. Liberation theology, to which Jackson was sympathetic, was spreading its roots in many black churches. The Black Panthers, who proclaimed a need for "Black Power", held a large conference right across the street from the Diamond Street Mennonite Church at the Episcopal Church of the Advocate. During this time the church responded to a community need for a child care facility by converting the now-unoccupied Bethany Home for the Elderly into a childcare center.

At the Liberty Bell - - , Homer Schrock,
Frances and Raymond Jackson - 1968

The broader Mennonite Church paid a lot of attention to Jackson because he was young, Mennonite, and black - an unusual combination in the church at that time. He was asked to be on committees, speak at conventions throughout the United States and in Africa. He was kept too busy to be the pastor he wanted to be. He and his family decided to take a pastorate in Columbus, Ohio at Burnside Mennonite Church in 1974.

The congregation again began their search for a pastor, specifically desiring a black Mennonite who could give half-time to ministry. No one was found in the congregation nor outside, so Roy Newswanger, long term pastor at Chester Mennonite Church and, at the time, on sabbatical, was asked to be interim pastor for one year while the search continued.

Freeman Miller seemed an unlikely pastor for a city church. Growing up Amish, he taught in an Amish school before he graduated from Ohio State University in Columbus. After marrying Naomi Peachey they volunteered a three-year term as teachers in Nigeria with Mennonite Central Committee. Returning to the States, he taught high school English in Columbus. He was at Eastern Mennonite Seminary in Harrisonburg, Virginia when he was first approached to consider the pastoral opening at Diamond Street. After a visit to Philadelphia and a number of conversations with those associated with the congregation, he was officially asked to fill the pastoral role. After discussion and prayer with his wife Naomi, he accepted.

The Millers' arrival in 1975 marked the beginning of a vigorous effort, rejuvenating old ideas that had lain dormant during the interim period. Their leadership excited the little congregation to attempt mammoth tasks only dreamed of before. He asked for a choir before there was a

Alice and Roy Newswanger - Interim pastor
at DSMC - 1974

Freeman and Naomi Miller Family - Gwen, Naomi,
Janelle, Freeman and Rhonda

director. The work of Tom Fitch is addressed in the first chapter of this history. Freeman took a public stance in support of inter-racial marriage, a stance in direct opposition to the purpose for opening the mission in 1935. During his pastorate there were several inter-racial couples in the congregation. The membership of 120 was a mix of African American and European American, with several African and other ethnicities represented.

Another large project was the response to a community desire to save the 1600 block of Diamond Street. The vacant buildings were scheduled for demolition and neighbors were asking that they be spared and rehabilitated. The church and community joined efforts and succeeded in securing the large three-story structure, 1632 West Diamond, from the Masons through the city's Gift Property Program in 1979. This gift allowed the church the space to begin full-scale efforts toward developing what is today the Diamond Street Community Center. By 1998, Eastern Mennonite Missions, backing

Raymond Jackson - storyteller

Raymond Jackson is a storyteller. Most likely this is what made him the well-loved preacher that he was at Diamond Street Mennonite Church when he

Raymond Jackson and Yolanda

became the first African-American preacher in the Philadelphia Mennonite Church. Raymond grew up in North Philadelphia and still claims it as his home, despite brief periods away in Atlanta, Georgia, where his wife Frances hails from, and Columbus, Ohio where he served for a brief time as minister. His mother, Easter Jackson, was one of the first members of Diamond Street Mennonite Church.

So if you ever have the opportunity to meet Raymond, ask for a story. Perhaps he'll share about his first encounter with Alma Ruth and Emma Rudy while playing ball outside his house. Or maybe he'll smile and tell you the story of his first-grade Sunday School teacher, Alleanor Jenkins who would lure him to the second row of the church with candy each Sunday. Possibly he'll laugh and tell you about Homer Schrock, "the dancing Amishman". Maybe he'll talk about his first attempts at preaching after hearing Luke Stoltzfus' use scripture verses on Sunday morning and dressing up and using "stories from the hood" to preach to friends when he got home. He might entertain you with former relationships with Black Panthers, drug addicts from the community, and Mennonites from Lancaster County. Whatever the story, you'll most likely walk away with the smile on your face and a little bit more hope in the church.

Diamond Street Mennonite Church also known as Diamond Street Community Center - 1990

the church in its revitalization program, granted the Diamond Street Mennonite Church ownership of the building and the congregation assumed responsibility in finishing the renovations.

A seventeen-member Board of Directors was formed with ten members from the church and seven members from the surrounding community. Monies for the restorations came from foundations, corporations, churches and individuals. Much of the work was done by volunteers and continued for several years. Services included a Seniors' program, a Wholistic Health Center, Youth Program, Social Services, Job Program, and rental for meeting space to the church. The various programs were staffed by both paid individuals and volunteers. Many of the programs discontinued for lack of funds. The most successful program was the Diamond Youth Program directed by Barbara (Allen) Baynard. She began in 1982 and continued into 1997. This was a continuation of the "Adventures in Brotherhood" begun under Pastor Homer Schrock. Another important program, coordinated by Frances Jackson, involved a food ministry for neighborhood folk that very often led to addressing further needs such as drug abuse, violence, crisis pregnancy, unemployment, illiteracy, and housing. Other early leaders in this program were James Allen, Jay Burkholder, Marie Clemens, and Rosa Clemens. They operated summer day camps for 75 to 80 children for 8 to 10 weeks. The mornings included Bible classes and craft activities. After lunch, the time was given to trips in the city and, on Fridays, to trips outside the city.

Bethany Child Care Center

Under the direction of Margaret Allen, Bethany Child Care Center was opened in the vacant 1910 Diamond Street building that had been Bethany Mennonite Home in 1972. EMM, who owned the building at 1910 West Diamond Street, approached the Diamond Street Mennonite Church about possible uses for the building. Pastor Raymond Jackson formed an interim Board and they began polling community residents for their opinions on possible options. The idea of creating a childcare center was determined to be the greatest need for the area. The interim Board quickly became the Bethany Child Care Center Board of Directors consisting of Pastor Raymond Jackson, Bishop Luke G. Stoltzfus, Robert Weaver, Joseph Lapp, Dale Weaver, and Margaret L. Allen. Bethany Child Care Center was officially opened in October of 1972. The Board was formally incorporated as a non-profit organization on April 29, 1980.

Margaret Allen - Director of Bethany Child Care Center

Bethany Child Care Center was originally the proprietor of only one building when it was first established, housing four classrooms of ten children and two teachers. Since then, the center has acquired two adjoining properties at 1908 and1912 West Diamond Street for the expanding after-school program and the pre-school program. In 1990, they were able to purchase a building and renovate it for an infant/toddler program.

Over the past 26 years, BCCC increased from thirty pre-school children to an early childhood development center which includes children from three months to age twelve. In a two and a half story brick building, the center houses eight infants, ten toddlers, forty-eight pre-schoolers, and twelve school-aged children. Bethany now has eighteen full-time and five part-time staff. Parent volunteers help with field trips and some persons who were students here in the early years, came back to the center as volunteers and later became permanent full-time staff.

Testimonies from Staff:

Betty Brooks - "I remember when Bethany was just 1 building with only four classrooms. Each class had ten children of mixed ages with two caregivers. The meals were the greatest (I

Betty Brooks - teacher with children at pool

thought that the parents came out mostly for the food). I remember when the 1912 building was renovated. I watched Bethany grow and I was carried with it. Then the third building was purchased and infants and toddlers came to Bethany. Yes, BCCC has changed."

Anne Blocker - "I have seen the change of our parents from young 20s to the very young teens. There have been changes in the Welfare system, which has put demands on Bethany's social services. We at Bethany have arisen to the challenge with computer programs to prepare our children for the future. We encourage and sometimes insist that parents get specialized medical care. We take time to talk to the parents letting them know that we are concerned about them as well as their children."

*Anne (White) Blocker
1983*

*Novellette Hylton
1999*

Novellette Hylton - "I came to Bethany as a VS worker with the Mennonite Church. Because of the VS persons, the staff became a mixed group culturally. The children learned that even though the color of one's skin was different, we are basically the same. I thank God for bringing me to Bethany where I have discovered my true gift in working with children. The community benefits and appreciates a place like BCCC, knowing that their children are safe and properly cared for by people who truly care about their children."

In 1987, Miller accepted a call to become EMM's Home Ministries Director. He worked out of an office in Philadelphia, spending one day a week in Salunga. This meant a change in pastoral leadership for Diamond Street. During the ten years of Miller's service, the multi-racial membership reached its highest point of 120.

After seventeen years of faithful service as assistant pastor and providing a stable leadership presence with integrity, Charles Baynard became the lead pastor for Diamond Street. In a recent interview he reflected on the good times at the Fellowship Meetings where other Mennonite Churches with African-American membership used to come together for a day of fellowship and worship. These meetings and the camping program for youth were the means by which young people learned to know others across the church. Some even met life companions in this way. This was the case for Asa and Vera Grimes who now attend Christian Life Mennonite Church. He also recalls the way the men annually prepared and served a meal at the church for the women on Mother's Day. Other people remember fondly the many deeply-moving pastoral prayers Pastor Charles often prayed during the Sunday morning worship times.

Baynard's emphasis was to reach the community and to re-focus the mission of the congregation toward becoming a more indigenous African-American church. One method of reaching the community was to transfer the food distribution from the Community Center to the church. Ed and Mattie (Cooper) Nikiema were the leaders for this program. They conducted Bible studies and prayer meetings for the forty to fifty people who came for food bags on Wednesday evenings. Currently there are at least seven people who attend the church as a result of initially coming to these events.

Summer Bible School - Earl Ridley, Ron Tinsley, Freeman Miller, Yolanda Jackson - 1984

Charles and Barbara Baynard Family -
Back row: Walter, Carl, Timothy, Benjamin, Barbara, Charles, Paul, "Peaches"

During the early 1990's at the Diamond Street congregation, a heightened degree of racial tension persisted within the church. Issues centered on how the church would interact with the community, as well as how whites and blacks would share leadership in church matters. Baynard's focus on becoming a more autonomous congregation for African Americans at times resulted in white members feeling excluded. Eventually, a number of families of both races left the church as a result of these conflicts. By 1995, membership dropped to a low of twenty-five to thirty people. Baynard's battle with several diseases also became an added burden to him. In 1996, after nine years as Senior Pastor at Diamond Street

Charles and Barbara
Baynard - 1995

Ed and Mattie Nikiema Family - Illya Johnson, (foster son), Mattie, Ed

Current Pastor Otis, and Carrlett Banks - 1998

Mennonite Church, Baynard left the pastorate, opting for early retirement status.* (see footnote)

At this time, Otis and Carrlett Banks became the interim pastoral couple for Diamond Street. Otis had been working for EMM Home Ministries as a specialist to African-American ministers. Otis sensed that the development of the church and its community center was a great challenge and opportunity. The congregation once again became more inter-racial with many students from nearby Messiah College, Philadelphia Campus, and Temple University attending. Also, more persons from the neighborhood attended and became members. Pastor Banks brought a renewed vision to the congregation, with an emphasis on both racial reconciliation and community development. His gentle, but firm, spirit and vibrant Biblical preaching continue to bless and encourage long-term and newer members alike.

Ephener Green - Director of Diamond Street Community Center - 1999

Since 1996, Pastor Banks and a committed group of elders and members have worked together to strengthen both the internal structure of the congregation and the community outreach. On weekday mornings, Pastor Banks and others in the church may be found walking the streets of the community, introducing themselves and the church to their neighbors. Ongoing renovations continue in the community center where Ephener Green directs a variety of programs including after-school tutoring services and computer training classes. Other projected programs will be added as grants are approved. In a low-income community that is severely affected by changes in government welfare funding, such programs provide a vital service to families in the neighborhood. Diamond Street Mennonite Church continues to provide a stable presence in the heart of North Philadelphia, while incorporating a theology based on both service and evangelism.

* Pastor Charles Baynard's health continued to decline after his retirement, leading to his death on June 16, 1999. Hundreds of people packed Diamond Street Mennonite Church at his Home-going service, giving testimony to his faithful ministry to Christ and the church over the years.

Oxford Circle Mennonite Church

During World War II there was a need for housing military service families at a minimal cost in Philadelphia. The need was supplied by building a village of approximately 600 one-story cement-block houses next to the Naval Depot in Northeast Philadelphia. Since the location was near a main street called Oxford Avenue, the village was named Oxford Village. The area provided affordable housing which attracted one Mennonite family who were members of Norris Square at the time. This family, Harry and Viva Reedel and their four children, moved to Oxford Village in 1945.

The Reedels soon discerned a need for religious teaching among the residents because there was a lack of church presence in the area. They slowly got to know neighboring families and began transporting some children to Norris Square Mennonite Church on Sunday mornings. This proved a big task as Norris Square was eight miles away on the other side of the city. By July 1946, Viva started gathering children in her backyard to tell Bible stories. Later, the first Bible School, with forty-nine children attending, was held in the homes of the Reedels and Alice Reeves, a widow with three sons. For the closing program a bus was chartered, and pupils and parents were transported to the Norris Square Mennonite Church. These activities created an increased interest in hearing Bible stories in the community. By the end of the summer, there was enough interest to start an afternoon Sunday School in the Reedel home in which there was an average attendance of twenty-four.

By September, as interest continued to increase, more help was needed, and the David Troyer family, of Wilmington, Delaware, was asked to assist. They traveled to Philadelphia by train each Sunday. Soon the services changed from Sunday afternoon to Sunday morning. Attendance continued to grow, and so some classes were held in Alice Reeves' home. A monthly religious paper called "The Way"

Harry and Viva Reedel Family - Eunice, Rhoda, Clemet, Harry, Viva, and Chris - 1950

was distributed door-to-door in the village. Youth groups from Mennonite Churches in Lancaster County helped to pass these out and afterwards held street meetings in the area.

Because of the growing interest, a lot for building a church was

Alice Reeves Family - Fred, Alice with David, Lynn

Oxford Circle Basement Church - 1950

found nearby and purchased by the Eastern Mennonite Mission Board. Ground was broken in November, 1948, for a basement church and was dedicated in February 1949. J. Paul Graybill and George R. Brunk II were speakers, and Henry Garber, EMM President, moderated at the dedication.

In August 1949, John Winters attended the Missionary Training Institute where he met Henry Garber, who later asked him to help with the work at Oxford Circle. After prayerful consideration, he and his wife, Ida, and family began to attend. John's first impression of Oxford Circle was not the best. He had to enter the church on boards laid across the mud. Inside, water had to be scooped up before any services could begin. This was a weekly task, and so the floor was always damp. One elderly lady always wore overshoes. John preached his first sermon there on November 20, 1949. Those attending that first service were George and Gladys (Sensenig) Weber, Laura Weber, Ruth Brendle, and the Reedel and Reeves families.

For the first year, the Reedels, who were responsible for the services, welcomed John into their home for lunch each Sunday. In the afternoons, Harry would show him around the village, and they would stop at homes where he had previous contacts. John was already an ordained deacon at Kinzer Mennonite Church, but he was not ordained as minister for Oxford Circle until December 1952.

John remembers Harry taking him to visit the Miller home. Martha Miller was an attendee and later became a member. After two years of high school in the city, friends of the church helped her attend Lancaster Mennonite High School where she graduated in 1959. After her mother's death, she became the Winters' foster daughter.

Martha (Miller) High - Graduation 1959, John and Ida Winters Family - Donald, Richard, Ida, Joyce, John - 1956

Elizabeth Patterson was another devout member. Her husband, an alcoholic, became a Christian on his

deathbed. She helped many in the village because of her life experiences. She sat on the last bench in the church and watched for children who misbehaved, often using her cane to remind them to be attentive.

Elizabeth Patterson 1950

After two years in the basement church, John requested that the upper part of the building be completed. This was granted by EMM, and the work was carried out with volunteer help. By the fall of 1951, the work was completed. A small apartment was included and used by the Winters family on weekends until 1953, when Laura Weber and Esther Clark, sister workers, moved into this apartment.

Laura Weber (Landis) had moved into Philadelphia in the winter of 1948-49. She was employed in a doctor's home and came to help at Oxford Circle on Sundays. Esther Clark was helping with Sunday School and Bible School as early as 1950. Laura and Esther were dedicated "sister workers" who did much home visitation. They would go on Sunday mornings to homes while the parents were still asleep, get the children out of bed, find clothes for them, wash their faces and bring them to church. They also ministered to many of the elderly in the community.

Completed church above basement - 1951

Sunday School Teachers - first row: Lois (Shirk) Hollinger, – , Laura (Weber) Landis, Esther Clark, Ida Winters, Evelyn (Leaman) Bair, Anna Mae Reist, Ruth Brendle, Gladys (Sensenig) Weber, second row: Clair Hollinger, Ivan Troxel, Paul White, John Winters, David Frederick, Robert Hershey, Norman Shirk, George Weber

Many others from Lancaster County helped in the work. Sunday School attendance rose to about 175. In 1950, Paul and Helen White came to assist and helped for a number of years in teaching and organizing. In June of 1954, the Glenn and Erla Ranck family began commuting from Bucks County, because they felt God calling them to do mission work in the city. Later they moved into the city and began a market business. They raised four children in Philadelphia. They served faithfully in the church until their deaths - Glenn in 1980 and Erla in 1994.

Carol (Stone) Reinford, as a child, lived across the street from the church. Later, after moving to Chester, she became a member and, with her mother's permission, came to live with Laura and Esther at Oxford Circle. She lived with them until she was married to Clyde Reinford in 1967. Laura continued to live in the apartment with Esther until 1977, when she went to

Glen and Erla Ranck Family - Glen, Erla, James, Karen, Kenneth, Donald - 1968

Crockett, Kentucky to teach school where the Reinford family was living at the time. After Laura left, Sharon (Weber) Lazarus lived in the apartment for a year until Sharon bought her own house where the two moved into together. When Sharon got married in 1987, Esther moved to Lancaster after more than thirty years of working with the church.

Carol (Stone) and Clyde Reinford Wedding day 1967

Throughout the 1950's, attendance at Oxford Circle continued to be primarily children and youth from the neighborhood, combined with Mennonites who had moved to the city from the country. By 1956, there were only 11 on the membership rolls, mostly Mennonites from outside the city, but Sunday School attendance averaged around 105 individuals, mostly children and youth[40]. The Housing Authority of Philadelphia razed about half of the units at Oxford Village in 1956. Many of the residents moved elsewhere. This greatly reduced the attendance at Sunday School and Bible School. By 1962, average attendance at the Sunday morning services had dropped to 55[41].

In 1958, John Winters resigned from his pastoral duties because of health reasons. In anticipation of this transition, the church had called a new pastor in June of 1957. Donald Wenger had been working at Norristown State Hospital to fulfill his conscientious objector obligations. He and his wife, Ruth (Hackman), were attending Oxford Circle where Donald, along with Glen Ranck and George Weber, were in the class for the ministry. Donald was chosen by lot to fill the pastoral role. The lot process involved the three male class members each choosing from three Bibles on a table. The one who chose the Bible with a scripture verse written on a piece of paper within (in this case Donald), was considered to be "chosen" by God to be the pastor.

Ruth Graybill: Oxford Circle Pillar

On a typical Sunday morning at the Oxford Circle Mennonite Church, amidst joyous celebratory music, one can peer across the diverse congregation and see an elderly Mennonite woman sitting quietly in her pew, bowing her head and gently lifting a hand upwards in praise. Ruth Graybill arrived in Philadelphia in 1950 after feeling a calling to a ministry to Jewish people. For the next fifty years, Ruth remained a dedicated church worker in the city. Since 1974, she has been a faithful member of Oxford Circle where her quiet presence serves as an inspiration to others in the church. Despite this calm demeanor, Pastor Leonard Dow describes Ruth as a "prayer warrior", who tells people "don't ask me to pray if you don't think that it will be answered".

During his pastorate, a house, 5902 Langdon Street, directly across the street from the church, was purchased as a parsonage. In the winter of 1961-62, the Wengers attended the Ontario Mennonite Bible School. Later that year they accepted a call to pastor in Manheim, Ontario.

Bishop Stoner Krady (retired from his Lancaster churches) had come to Philadelphia to minister at the Messianic Fellowship Center at 613 South 48th Street in 1962. They had a second floor apartment and shared the house with Ruth Graybill, Miriam Stoltzfus and Ada Myer, and later with Amos and Naomi Harnish. Since services at the Center were held in the afternoon and evening, Brother and Sister Krady attended Oxford Circle for Sunday morning worship. In the absence of a resident pastor, Brother Krady served as pastor for four years, until his death in November 1966.

Francis and Pastor Stoner Krady
1962 - 1966

In August of 1966, George Weber was ordained as a minister by the new bishop, Luke Stoltzfus. George and Gladys (Sensenig) Weber had been teaching Sunday School at Oxford Circle since 1948, before they were married. They began dating in 1949 and married in 1950. Each had moved to Philadelphia and found work in the city. They continued to be involved at Oxford Circle until he was called into 1W (conscientious objection) service in the South. They returned to Philadelphia in 1956 and later moved into the parsonage on Langdon Street when the Wengers left for Ontario. After serving as pastor from 1966 to 1971, they went to Rosedale Bible College in Ohio for a term of Bible School. While there a call came for them to pastor in Tamaqua, Pennsylvania. They sensed God's leading and moved in June of 1971.

George and Gladys Weber Family
George, Gladys, Lois Mary Ann

When George and Gladys went to Rosedale, Jacob (former pastor of Norris Square Mennonite Church) and Anna Frederick came to Oxford Circle to fill the pastoral role for a time. They served from January 1971 to June 1972. During this time, Jacob asked Kenneth Bucher to come to Oxford Circle to assist with Sunday School and Cottage meetings. Kenneth, as a single young man, moved into the now vacant parsonage at 5902 Langdon Street. Kenneth came to Philadelphia in Voluntary Service in September of 1971. He was a registered nurse and worked at Presbyterian/University of Pennsylvania Hospital in West Philadelphia. In March of 1973, Kenneth married Evelyn Brandt whose VS time had overlapped with Ken's for three months in 1971. He was ordained in 1974 and continued to serve as pastor until 1980. For about three years, between 1977 and 1980, he shared the pastoral responsibilities with Jim Leaman.

Jim and his wife Beth, like Kenneth, had also come to Philadelphia as voluntary service workers in 1969. After serving as youth worker, assistant pastor, and lead pastor at Norris Square Mennonite Church before its transition to Iglesia Menonita Arca de Salvacion, Jim and Beth left the city for three years to attend seminary at Eastern Mennonite University. They were invited to return in 1977 so that Jim could serve as a co-pastor with Kenneth. The two worked side by side and shared most of the pastoral duties, greatly aided by the continuing work of the sister workers, Laura Weber and Esther Clarke.

Ken and Evie Bucher Family
Evie holding Kendra, Ken with Keith
and Kevin - 1980

Out of the vision of a church growth team in the late 1970's, a difficult decision was made to change the focus from busing children to Sunday School services to moving towards a more family-oriented ministry. The new vision came to fruition, but it happened slowly and gradually over a number of years. In June of 1980, Kenneth moved with his family to Lancaster County where he became pastor at Manheim Mennonite Church. Ten days later the church grieved the death of long-time worker Glenn Ranck.

Losses in church membership like this had a large impact on small urban congregations, particularly because there were few men involved in the church at this time. Pastor Jim found himself searching for direction, "The night of Glenn's death, I sat in his youth Sunday School classroom and cried my heart out to God. What were his purposes through all of this?"[42].

Don and Dorothy Schmucker, who had been attending Diamond Street Mennonite Church, affirmed an invitation to join the team at Oxford Circle. The church continued to pray for more men and for couples to become a part of the Oxford Circle fellowship. Gradually, their dreams of a more family-centered congregation began to be realized. People came, some to stay and others to eventually move on. Some were blue collar, others professionals. Various church backgrounds and a sprinkling of different cultures were represented. VSers, Youth Evangelism Service participants (YESers) from the Philadelphia YES training center, and also college and graduate students became part of the congregation, many for short periods of time. These were usually mutually nourishing relationships, although it was difficult to say goodbye so often.

In the late '70's a daily summer day camp was started. Kids came from the neighborhood to study the Bible, do crafts, sing, and take day trips to city museums and Lancaster County farms and other sites like the Strasburg Railroad. In later years, day camp down-sized to summer club, but also expanded to after-school club a couple of afternoons a week, with YESers assisting during their training in Philadelphia. Treva Stutzman and John McGraw gave much leadership in later years.

V.S. unit at NSMC - Jim Lehman, Elsie Eberly, Dennis Purcell, Naomi (Hostetter) Sensenig, Dave Landis, Beth (Kling) Leaman and Jim Leaman - 1970

Sweetheart Banquet 1989 - Don and Dorothy Schmucker, Debbie Delegalis, Luke Stoltzfus, George Delegalis and Verna (Shirk) Wyant

The Oxford Circle leadership during the 1980's considered relationships with other churches to be important. They shared in annual Good Friday afternoon services and later, on Palm Saturdays, walks replete with donkey and palm branches and worship along the way. The church building was shared with two other Mennonite congregations for a number of years into the early 1990's. The Oxford Circle congregation met on Sunday morning, Bethany House of Worship (an Asian Indian membership) met in the afternoon, and Iglesia Menonita Comunidad de Amor gathered in the evening. Occasionally all three congregations worshipped together.

Tim Bentch - An Oxford Circle Testimony

Probably like many others, I came to Oxford Circle hurting, searching, and in need. What I found was a curiously-matched family that accepted me as I was, and gently encouraged and challenged me.

During early morning prayers, I learned about the quiet power of prayer from the examples of Ruth Graybill, Jim and Beth Leaman, Galen Burkholder, and others. I experienced real Christian community in our little celebrations where I saw friendship and love crossing many barriers of age, and embracing a diverse spectrum of people. My favorite was the annual Valentine's banquet when old and young, single and married, convened to enjoy our gift of love for each other by singing, playing games and eating little heart-shaped cookies - an unlikely happening in today's world. I rejoiced in seeing the miracle taking place in my own life as fear and doubt were replaced by hope and faith.

Tim Bentch attended Oxford Circle from 1985 to 1987 while in graduate school in Philadelphia.

In 1988, the congregation faced a crisis in a construction project of turning the church sanctuary around so that they would have a small foyer at the rear of the sanctuary, with a new entrance. The contractor's work was very sub-par, and the church had overpaid thousands of dollars for work not completed. The congregation struggled. Should they sue the contractor, a "brother Christian" from another church? They decided to use mediation, which was only partially successful. In the end, Mennonite Disaster Service volunteers completed the job. They had a simple but beautiful sanctuary, and Pastor Jim reflects that, "we learned about peacemaking in a tough situation".[43]

Jim and Beth Leaman Family -
Todd Bowman, Marie (Leaman) Bowman,
Tim Leaman, Beth (Kling) and Jim Leaman.

The annual live, outdoor nativity pageant became an Oxford Circle tradition for sixteen years. The pageant, held in early December, was the brainchild of Sharon Weber Lauzus, who originated it, gathered costumes, and for a number of years directed it. Church musician Erla Ranck shared her ministry in the pageant. Neighborhood Bible studies, Saturday morning men's breakfasts, all-night prayer meetings, youth outreach, church retreats at Camp Men-O-Lan near Quakertown, taking turn at a soup kitchen, developing a worship team, and "Making Peace with Your Past" classes (led by Beth Leaman) were all part of Oxford Circle Mennonite Church life in their efforts to draw more families and young adults into the congregation. The congregation continued to shift towards more of a family focused atmosphere to compliment the youth work, led primarily by Treva Stutzman during the 80's and 90's.

Vandy, Lynn, and Bethany Parks 1998

The Gonzalez family: Keeping the Church Alive

Henry and Maribelys Gonzalez have attended Oxford Circle since 1998. Both had attended Hispanic Pentecostal churches in the past and were looking for a change of pace. They, along with their sons Jeremy and Christopher, provide a testimony to the importance of committed lay members in the success of the church. Maribelys volunteers hours each week to the Sunday bulletin and other administrative task, often stopping by the church to ask the Pastor Leonard Dow what tasks need to be done. Henry is a member of the church worship team, playing drums and helping the team to fuse together a number of diverse musical worship styles. He also serves as the youth pastor in the congregation, a critical aspect as the church continues to attract young couples. Together, the Gonzalez family represent the new generation of committed believers at Oxford Circle.

Pastoral Transitions

During the summer of 1997, Pastor Jim requested that he and his wife Beth be allowed a year-long "Sabbath", a sabbatical-like year away from the church to discern future direction, beginning in 1998. Bishop Freeman Miller assisted the congregation in setting up a ministry team made up of Larry Fahnestock, Leonard Dow, and Vandy Parks to help coordinate church business and worship during the pastor's absence. Vandy Parks, a former member of Oxford Circle who had been pursuing church-planting efforts in Northeast Philadelphia, agreed to serve as the interim pastor. This led the congregation toward a more intentional team ministry effort as others members were also asked to fill various roles. In June of 1998, Pastor Jim asked to be permanently released as pastor, sensing that he and Beth had completed their ministry at Oxford Circle. Vandy Parks gave word that he would not consider the long-term pastoral position, and so the ministry team quickly set up a search for another pastor.

After interviewing several candidates from a nation-wide search, the church decided that it would be most appropriate to find somebody not only with prior urban experience, but ideally also somebody who knew the city of Philadelphia. The pool for such candidates was not large. During this time, Leonard Dow, an Oxford Circle member who was working in the banking industry, began to sense a calling to the ministry and away from banking. He approached Bishop Miller who encouraged

Leonard to pursue this calling. Many in the Philadelphia area already knew of Leonard's gifts for working with people and organizations. People within the church and other Philadelphia Mennonite church pastors had already approached him about the possibility of this type of career change. Upon further prayer and reflection, Leonard submitted his name to the pastoral search committee who affirmed the decision, and Leonard was officially welcomed as lead pastor by January of 1999. In keeping with a continued emphasis on team ministry, Pastor Leonard's position is half-time and Vandy Parks also puts in volunteer time as assistant pastor. Currently Leonard also works as half-time program coordinator for Mennonite Central Committee's Philadelphia Service Unit, and coordinates the work of Kingdom Builders, a city-wide coordinating effort of the Philadelphia Mennonite churches.

Leonard Dow Family - Rosalie (Rolon), Carmella, Leonard Dow - 1999

The neighborhood demographics are rapidly changing with more Latino and African-American families moving into the neighborhood, and a diverse, multi-ethnic congregation has begun to emerge in the late 1990's under the leadership of Pastor Leonard. When Leonard, who is African American, and his wife Rosalie, who is Hispanic, first visited the church in the early 90's, they found a congregation of all white individuals where they were two of the youngest people in attendance. Both current and past leadership feel that a new day is dawning at Oxford Circle with the emergence of this multicultural congregation. The members hope that this is a sign of reconciliation in the surrounding community as well.

Mennonite Witness Among Jewish People in Philadelphia

Fifty years ago Mennonites in Lancaster County, Pennsylvania were gathering at Vine Street Mennonite Church in Lancaster city to hear about prophecy related to Israel and to pray for witness among Jewish people. One of those Mennonites was Ruth Graybill. Jewish people from nearby cities vacationed in the Graybill home in the small town of New Holland . Ruth's uncle had a concern for Jewish people and a keen interest in Biblical prophecy. Ruth worked in a cheese plant owned by a Jewish man. In 1950, she moved to Philadelphia in a response to God's call to witness among Jewish people[44].

Ruth visited with Jewish women in their homes. She was assisted by Ada Myer, who provided childcare for a Jewish family. Olive Lucas came from New York, joined in the Jewish witness and joined the Mennonite Church. Other single sister workers, Miriam Stoltzfus and Mabel Brubaker, were partners with Ruth in this witness in later years. Ruth worked several years in West Philadelphia, for a while sharing with Stoner and Frances Krady a house known as the Messianic Fellowship Center. It had been purchased at first by Daniel Weaver from Lancaster County. Daniel went regularly to South 4th Street in Philadelphia to witness to Orthodox Jewish butchers. With Daniel's "Pennsylvania Dutch"(low German) and the businessmen's Yiddish, they were able to communicate. For a dozen years or more in the 1950's and 1960's, Jewish and Gentile believers gathered for fellowship meetings on Sunday afternoons at the Messianic Fellowship Center on South

Miriam Stoltzfus, Ruth Graybill, and Mabel Brubaker - 1963

48th Street. Some other Mennonite workers who participated were Walter Shirk, Amos and Naomi Harnish, and Donald and Dorothy Schmucker. Stoner Krady mentored Herb Zwickel, a Jewish student who came to the city. Herb later developed his own ministry elsewhere. Ruth Graybill helped to recruit George and Doris Gruen (of the Christian and Missionary Alliance) to Philadelphia, to witness among Jewish youth.

After Stoner Krady died, Bishop Luke and Miriam Stoltzfus moved into the Messianic Fellowship Center. Luke was active with what became the Shofar Committee of Lancaster Mennonite Conference and the Fellowship of Christian Testimonies to the Jews. Luke Stoltzfus and Herb Links of the Messianic Center on Chestnut Street, were mentors to a young Mennonite engineering student, Garry Denlinger, who later went to Israel to work as an engineer and later became involved in ministry there.

Mennonites came from Lancaster to help with the street meetings that were held as a witness to Jewish people in West Philadelphia and to distribute the pamphlet "Ha 'or"(the Light) in the Overbrook section of Philadelphia where the Beth Yeshua Messianic Synagogue is located. Also, the Korner Reading Room was operated for about ten years in the Lower Northeast part of the city. However, the vision for it to be an outreach to Jewish persons did not materialize. Ruth Graybill, Mabel Brubaker, and Miriam Stoltzfus lived and worked there, also using it as a base for Jewish home visitation. Often in the afternoons, Mabel would stay at the Reading Room while Ruth and Miriam visited families.

In the late 1970's, Jim Leaman became involved in Jewish witness in Philadelphia on a small scale. He participated in various capacities with the Shofar Committee of Lancaster Mennonite Conference. Shofar was an advocacy group for witness among Jewish people and the promotion of positive attitudes towards Jewish people in order to work against anti-Semitism. The Shofar Committee sponsored Jim in writing the book "Faith Roots - Learning from and Sharing Witness with Jewish People", published by Evangel Press of Nappanee, Indiana in 1993. Jim has served at various times in the leadership and witness of JOPPA (Jewish Outreach Partnership in the Philadelphia Area). The Shofar Committee, in 1997, disbanded the committee and "passed the mantle" of its vision to the whole Lancaster Mennonite Conference.

Over these forty years of ministry in Philadelphia, perhaps less than a dozen Jewish persons can be named who came to faith through Mennonite witness in Philadelphia. Many more were most likely touched in one way or another through the outreach. What originated as an evangelistic mission toward Jewish people in Philadelphia slowly evolved over the years to one of also discovering the common history and heritage that Jews and Mennonites hold in common. Those who continue this work, such as Ruth Graybill, and those who follow in her footsteps, still believe that a witness of Christianity among Jewish people is the call of the Gospel.

The Later Years:
Lancaster Conference in Philadelphia
- Growth and Diversity

The three oldest Lancaster Conference congregations in Philadelphia provided an important groundwork for the growth of the remaining congregations that have been planted since the 1960's. It is questionable as to whether these newer congregations have actually been products of the Lancaster Conference or whether the conference only acted as a conduit through which visionary church evangelists, many from non-Mennonite backgrounds, could have the structure and support necessary for church planting in urban areas. As we will see below, the answer is both. Most of the newer congregations in Philadelphia were developed as Mennonite church leaders identified unchurched areas of the city, invited appropriate potential church-planters for these neighborhoods, and then freed these newer leaders to do the work without a lot of church constraint.

The transition into this new era of church growth in Philadelphia was most characterized by two changes in church structure. First, the ordination of Luke Stoltzfus as Bishop of the Philadelphia District in 1965 replaced the traditionalist stance of former Bishop J. Paul Graybill with a more progressive and flexible leadership style. Stoltzfus though still not willing to betray the dominant church values and practices, was much more willing to listen and be flexible than Graybill. Over time, this led to a unique combination of urban evangelism accompanied by an identified importance on self-determination for oppressed racial groups. Mattie Nikiema, who was a teenager when Stoltzfus first arrived in Philadelphia, describes this leadership style:

> We used to discuss these things (cultural differences) with Luke Stoltzfus. He was very patient with us and always allowed us questions. I give him that, that he allowed us our questioning
> ... I think that we both came to understand that, although we have to have principles, not all of these old patterns were necessary.

Perhaps more important than Stoltzfus' individual initiative though, was the broader changes taking place in the Mennonite church at this time which allowed Bishop Stoltzfus to confront traditional ideas that may have been too difficult to deal with during Graybill's years. Kniss[45] describes the years between 1935 and 1958 as a time when sectarian boundaries of the Mennonite Church were beginning to be broken down, even in the traditional Lancaster Conference where "a powerful bishop board maintained its traditionalist grip for longer than the bishops in other conferences." As the broader church moved toward a more egalitarian mode of leadership, Stoltzfus was also able to loosen his grip on tradition in a way that Graybill was not able to. In fact, because of a deep desire for urban church planting in the broader church and an increasing consciousness of cultural sensitivity in religious practice, Philadelphia Mennonites were often allowed the freedom to break traditional norms where others could not, leading the way to greater flexibility in practice and ideas. Raymond Jackson, the first African-American pastor at Diamond Street, recalls a Lancaster County pastor encouraging him to wear a tie, (which was frowned upon at the time), to a conference gathering, thinking that he would be able to get away with it, which would then open the doors for others to wear ties.

Just as the beginning of the century was greatly influenced by mass migration to the United States, so also was the 1960's and 1970's. In 1965, the U.S. repealed immigration laws that had previously restricted Asian immigrants to the U.S. Other factors led to more doors opening for immigrants from Latin American countries[46]. Many of these immigrants looked to Northern U.S. cities, such as Philadelphia, for job opportunities. Luke Stoltzfus, Bishop of the Philadelphia District, and staff at Eastern Mennonite Missions took notice of these changes. They began to rethink their vision for the future of the Mennonite Church in Philadelphia, and imagined the structural and cultural implications of these changes for the church. Bishop Stoltzfus wrote in a 1973 paper for an Eastern Mennonite College sociology course:

> For a church which is predominantly German-American, language barriers loom large when outreach is attempted among Puerto Ricans. Cultural barriers are equally large. When the church attempts outreach among Jews, the conventional methods of Sunday School, Sunday morning worship and Bible schools are hardly suitable. When a predominately white-American church attempts church building in the black community today the history of white domination of blacks is very significant. The meanings to all the above groups of such things as race, color, prejudice, discrimination, social class, etc... are going to vary and have implications for church building[47].

The face of the Lancaster Conference Philadelphia District was to change its look dramatically in the next three decades, from three churches prior to 1965 to fourteen churches by 1999. The uncommon diversity of the District is apparent in the fact that these congregations speak eleven different languages in their church services. Diamond Street Mennonite Church would branch out by sending one of its assistant pastors, Daryl Wallace, to Second Mennonite, an Eastern District Church, and another, James Dennis, to pastor the newer Christian Life Church in Philadelphia. Ted Yao, an independent-minded Chinese church-planter, set the stage for three Asian churches to begin. As other new immigrant communities grew in the city, EMM identified church planters with Mennonite backgrounds such as Sanjeevara Vangore and Quang Tran. Others who were asked to begin churches had no prior experience with Mennonites and knew little about the Anabaptist faith, such as Sarin Lay and Lemuel So. Still others had already started their church-planting efforts and teamed up with EMM for institutional support – all under a Mennonite identity. The growth of so many churches with so little Anabaptist background was facilitated by Bishop Stoltzfus, and later Freeman Miller who was ordained Bishop of the Philadelphia District in 1994, when Stoltzfus retired. Another crucial step in the process was the hiring of Leonard Burkholder by EMM as a coach for non-English speaking congregations. Burkholder has worked with a number of Philadelphia churches over the past years, negotiating cultural and religious boundaries that often conflict.

Leonard and Anna Mary Burkholder Family - Nathan, Stephen, Leonard, Dawn, Anna Mary, and Timothy - 1997

Philadelphia Mennonite Council

In an effort to create a more organized Mennonite presence in the city, the Philadelphia Mennonite Council was started in the early 1970's. In October 1971, a group of about a dozen Philadelphia Mennonites met to discuss how they might work together better. They represented Philadelphia Mennonite Churches, Lancaster (LMC) and Franconia (FMC) Mennonite Conferences, Mennonite Board of Missions (MBM), and Mennonite Student Services (MSS). The meeting was largely initiated by the encouragement of Ray Horst of MBM and partly because of FMC's involvement in Inter-Faith Realty Company (IRC). IRC had some properties in North Philadelphia of which they wanted to dispose. They were pursuing whether these properties could be used by the Mennonite Church in its ministry in the city. At this time, there were three Old Mennonite (OM) churches in the city and three General Conference (GC) Mennonite churches. Mennonite Student Services had been active in Philadelphia for many years and had, up to this time, occasionally brought together Mennonites in the city.

At the meeting, Richard Detweiler of FMC challenged the churches as to their vision for Philadelphia. This resulted in the forming of the Philadelphia Mennonite Coordinating Committee, a group of five persons assigned with the task of determining the course of action of future meetings. There were several meetings in the next year during which the Philadelphia Mennonite Council (PMC) was formed, a long-term coordinating committee for the Philadelphia-Chester District. This consisted of the pastors of all OM and GC churches, Mennonite-related agencies such as Messiah College, MSS, VS units, and Germantown Mennonite Corporation. For many years, PMC functioned primarily as a coordinating council rather than an administrative one. After several years it was incorporated. A number of joint projects were generated through the PMC. A van was purchased to transport students from Philadelphia to Christopher Dock Mennonite High School. The Christian School Committee (CSC) developed out of the PMC and still exists today. CSC's primary function was to collect money for scholarships for church families who desired to send their children to an elemntary Christian Day School. The LINK, a 10 month/year newsletter, was published by the PMC office. It served as a newspiece to help the Mennonites be aware of each other. The PMC also sponsored meetings for fellowship or worship once or twice a year, such as at Christmas or Easter. When persons wanted to hear a Philadelphia voice or opinion, they often turned to PMC for that. In the early 1980s, PMC hosted the Region V Assembly of the Mennonite Church. PMC also managed receiving and distributing food bags for the Mennonite Central Committee. About twelve churches or agencies were involved in this ministry.

In 1976, The Meetinghouse was created as an alternative peace witness while most of society was celebrating a violent time of war, the Revolutionary War. It was located near Independence National Park. It continued for about three years and then discontinued largely because of financial considerations.

PMC was also involved in the beginning of West Philadelphia Mennonite Fellowship. The church was initiated by PMC as a Bible study group in the West Philadelphia area, originally meeting in the home of Luke and Miriam Stoltzfus. Half of the original sixteen participants were former members at Diamond Street Mennonite Church who lived in West Philadelphia. Diane Stitt (Melchert) led the group through its formative stages. David Greiser joined the pastoral team around the time that public worship services began. The core of sixteen is now a church of about 100 adults and children. Pastors Libby Caes and Fred Kauffman have served the congregation in the 1990s. Although the congregation was established through a joint effort of both the Lancaster and Franconia Conferences, it chose to become a member of the Franconia Conference in their early years.

PMC has struggled to maintain its existence since its beginning. The financial assistance of conferences was very necessary. PMC underwent several evaluations in its more than twenty years of existence. Many do not want to return to a time when Philadelphia Mennonites did not have a structure for mutual awareness, interaction, and encouragement. In 1998, the PMC was revived as Kingdom Builders. Coordinated by Leonard Dow, pastor at Oxford Circle Mennonite Church, Kingdom Builders seeks to coordinate the work of the different Mennonite congregations and conferences in the greater Philadelphia area. By far the most significant collaborative effort in this regard has been the development of the Philadelphia Mennonite High School which we describe in the final pages of this book.

As you will read, the story of the newer Philadelphia District churches, at least as told here, is a story of their leaders. Over time, this will likely evolve into a fuller picture of lay member involvement, but new churches tend to rely heavily on their leaders. The Philadelphia District is still in the process of becoming a unified body. A quick glance at the District displays a multi-cultural context that is extremely rare among church denominations in the United States. A closer look reveals that these different ethnic groups are still, for the most part, segregated between congregations. A few of the congregations are working intentionally toward a more multi-cultural attendance and membership, but cultural and language barriers often stand in the way. The tension between providing a safe space for cultural worship and modeling the diverse Kingdom of God within particular congregations will be one of the challenges for the Philadelphia District in the 21st Century.

The second section of the book describes the growth of the thirteen newer congregations in the Philadelphia District. We also include a summary of the development of the Philadelphia Mennonite High School as written by Arbutus Sider, and a look into the future by Bishop Freeman Miller.

Bethany House of Worship

Pastor Sanjeevarao Vangore was born in India in the home of a Mennonite Brethren pastor. His father was a teacher at the Shemshabad Mennonite Brethren Seminary. When he finished high school, he asked his father what vocation he should follow. His father's response was that he wanted him to become the Lord's servant. Vangore knew what hardships would lie ahead if he went into Christian service. Ministers were not paid well in India and it would be hard to support a family. He worked as a supervisor on the railroad while attending college. He finished with both a bachelor's degree and a law degree. He married in India while his wife Surya was in medical school. A nephew wrote to him about a seminary in South Carolina where he could study for the ministry. When he applied, he was granted a full scholarship by the Erskine Theological Seminary. He came to America in 1973 and graduated with a Master of Theology degree in 1976.

Sanjeevarao and Surya Vangore - 1999

Surya was in London at this time. Since the community in South Carolina was in dire need of doctors, they arranged for her coming and obtained an immigrant visa for both her and Vangore. She arrived in 1975. Because Surya's training was in India she needed to take additional training in the U.S. That is when they moved to Philadelphia to do her residency at Temple University Hospital.

They lived near Third and Wyoming Streets in Philadelphia and began witnessing to their neighbors who were also from India. By first establishing friendships, and then talking to them about their faith, some of these families who had been Hindu now became Christians. Other immigrant families from India gravitated to this church because they could understand one of their own countrymen better than the American-style preachers. Pastor Vangore explains the process, "They said, 'brother, when you teach the word of God, we understand it nicely, but we are not able to understand it in these American churches. Why not have our own church?'. So I said to them, 'It's not our will. We must find the Lord's will. And so let's pray.' And for one month we prayed. When we came back together we knew that it was the Lord's will and we named our church Bethany House of Worship." This was the beginning of their congregation which was registered with the state in 1980. The name, Bethany House of Worship was given to them by Bakht Singh , a well-known evangelist in India.

Shortly after arriving in Philadelphia, Pastor Vangore met Jim Leaman, then pastor of Oxford Circle Mennonite Church. Pastor Vangore wanted to continue the Mennonite heritage that his father had started (his grandfathers were Baptist and he is not certain how his father came into contact with the Mennonite church) and asked for licensure from the Mennonite Church. For the first two years, Pastor Vangore was licensed by the Franconia Conference, but has since transferred his license to Lancaster Conference. The congregation itself is still not officially affiliated with any Mennonite conference, as it continues to discern whether it wants to attach itself to any denominational identity or to remain non-denominational.

The congregation of thirty-eight members has included persons of Hindu, Muslim, and Christian background. The primary language is Telegu, but since not all use that language, preaching and hymn-singing are in English which all understand. Pastor Vangore encourages participants to pray in their own language and so opens prayer time is a mix of dialects. The congregation has purchased a property recently at 1070 West 69th Avenue. Now they no longer need to move around in rental facilities as they had before. Attendance on Sunday mornings fluctuates between twenty and fifty, and as many as one hundred attend on special services. Pastor Vangore continues as the primary leader and is assisted by a youth leader, Ryan Khan.

The Vietnamese Mennonite Church

Quang and Tam Tran have pastored the Vietnamese Mennonite Church from its inception in 1982. Both Quang and Tam were raised in pastor's homes of the Christian and Missionary Alliance Church in Vietnam. Quang's parents ministered in the South and Tam's parents ministered in the North. In 1954, when Vietnam was divided, Tam's family moved south. After serving two years with the military, Quang worked for the Navigators, an evangelical scripture-distributing group, and later for the Vietnam Christian Service, an organization supported by the Mennonite Church, the Lutheran Church, and Church World Service. So although Quang and Tam knew the Mennonites when they were married in 1958, they did not begin working for the Vietnam Mennonite mission until 1965. The American Bible Society and the Southern Baptists asked them to help in their work, but after much prayer Quang chose to work with the Mennonites because he admired the way of life of the Mennonite missionaries.

They worked for ten years in Gia Dinh a small village not far from Saigon. He was ordained by the Mennonite mission in 1969. It was difficult to pastor the church during those years when young people had to go to the army and the church taught them not to kill. If they refused they were imprisoned.

In 1975, the Lancaster Mennonite Conference invited Pastor Quang to represent Asia in the Spring Assembly. He and Don Sensenig visited the families who had sent missionaries to Vietnam. He planned to

Quang and Tam Tran - Wedding reception at Chinese Restaurant - Quang, Tam, Mrs. Chau, Shirley Dich, Ben Yao - 1988

return after that, but in communication with his wife, they decided that he should stay in the U.S. because of the heavy fighting in Vietnam. She and their four children flew out of Saigon on a military transport plane in April of 1975. Although she wanted to bring her widowed father with her, the missionaries who helped with her escape would only bring her and the children. They had no time to bring any personal possessions. They spent a month travelling and in refugee quarters until their reunion with Quang at the MCC guest house in Akron, Pennsylvania.

After living in Goshen, Indiana for six months, Quang was invited back to Akron to work with MCC in a program to settle refugees in the U.S. Some of these families wanted to know more about Christianity, so Quang set up Bible studies in homes, and later at the Ephrata Mennonite Church on Sunday afternoons. Meanwhile, in Philadelphia, Luke and Miriam Stoltzfus were becoming aware of an expanding Vietnamese immigrant population within the area of the city where Miriam worked in the public schools. Luke, as Bishop of the Philadelphia District, approached Eastern Mennonite Missions in Lancaster with a request to explore the possibility of mission work among this immigrant community. Quang and Tam Tran were the likely candidates to lead such an outreach. In a small town like Ephrata there was little opportunity for expansion, so when asked to move to Philadelphia to plant a church for Vietnamese refugees in July 1982, they accepted.

They rented an apartment and tried to make friends within the Vietnamese community. Most of the Vietnamese immigrants came from Buddhist or Confucianist backgrounds and practiced various forms of ancestor worship. They could not find any Vietnamese Christians until several

Tuyen Nguyen: Non-violence at work

Tuyen Nguyen says it is very important to present the Gospel in the mother tongue of the hearers. He became a Christian in Vietnam, but he learned much more of the way of Christ when he came to the Vietnamese Mennonite Church in Philadelphia. For five years after meeting Mennonites, Tuyen struggled with the peace position. Once, when he was in front of the sanctuary at Vietnames Mennonite, a young man came running into the church, chased by another man with a gun (although Tuyen did not see the gun). Tuyen told the young man to come and stand behind him, so that Tuyen was a human shield for him. Then the gunman left. The next Sunday the gunman (no gun this time) came and sat beside Tuyen, apologizing for his behavior the previous Sunday. Today, Tuyen says that this story demonstrates the value of living a life-style of peace.

months later when they met a family that was baptized in an American church that sponsored them. For about one year the Tran family had meetings in their home every Friday evening with friends who wanted to know more about Christianity. They taught English classes and began services in rented facilities in September 1983.

Tam began working as an Aide in the ESOL classes (English for Speakers of Other Languages) at the H.C. Lea public elementary school at 47th and Locust Streets in Philadelphia. Later she became the Home and School Coordinator for the Asian student population. At this time, the 1500-member student body was one-third Asian. Her work was a very great help to the School District and afforded her entrance into the many Asian homes in the community.

They also rented an office in a large apartment building on South 48th Street, where many Vietnamese families lived. They used this office as a base to provide social services to the Vietnamese community, including after-school classes for children, as well as help for families in regard to housing, welfare, and medical assistance.

They continued the Sunday worship services renting space in three different locations from 1983 to 1990, sometimes sharing space with West Philadelphia Mennonite Fellowship. The group had grown from 20 to over 100 in those years. Congregation members were diverse in income and education, from welfare recipients to those with graduate degrees. They not only came from Philadelphia, but also from New Jersey and Delaware. There were Amerasian teenagers, whose fathers were American soldiers. There was quite a mixture; but Pastor Quang says that in Christ Jesus we are one and so he presented the Gospel in his sermons to those with little education as well as the highly educated.

District Leaders Meeting - Sarin Lay, Tuyen Nyguen and Richard Hwang (assistants in Vietnamese Mennonite Church) standing: Sing Kin So and Lemuel So - 1999

The group felt a need for a church building of their own since as refugees they had to move many times in the last 15 years. In November 1990, they celebrated a Thanksgiving feast at their newly renovated church building at 63rd and Woodland Ave. Much of the extensive repair was done by members of the congregation. Membership stands at 150, with an average attendance of 120 - 150. On special occasions, a capacity crowd of 200 fills the auditorium. Pastor Quang continues to give leadership to the congregation with the help of a leadership group. Although he preaches in his native Vietnamese language, a translator is always provided to English-speaking visitors. Their church is now planting "daughter" churches in South Philadelphia and in Delaware.

Love Truth Chinese Mennonite Church

In 1987, Lemuel So, a student at Canadian Theological Seminary, received a call from Freeman Miller, (Director of Eastern Mennonite Mission's Home Ministries Department) at the time, to inquire about his interest in a church plant among the Chinese immigrant community in Philadelphia. Although So knew very little about Mennonites at the time and had never been to Philadelphia before, he felt that the call to come visit the city was pre-arranged many years before. Approximately ten years prior, while still in his native Hong Kong, Pastor So had had a vision that he was being called to Philadelphia. At this time, he had no idea that a city of Philadelphia ever existed in the United States. He assumed that the dream was making some allusion to the church of Philadelphia in Revelations 3. He and his wife Leona went to visit the city. They were impressed by the warmth of Freeman Miller, as well as their stay at the home of Luke and Miriam Stoltzfus. But they were not so impressed with the situation. Two years earlier, Ted Yao had begun a ministry to the Chinese community in the basement of his home in the Logan area which Yao called the Logan Chinese Mennonite Church. There were very few Chinese immigrants who actually lived in this area.

Lemuel and Leona So Family - Joseph, Rebecca, back: Leona and Lemuel - 1997

The So couple saw a picture of urban distress that they were not accustomed to and were uncertain as to whether they were the right people for the position. On the plane on their way back to Canada, Lemuel prayed hard for discernment. Today he comments on this journey back, "I felt as if I was Jonah avoiding Nineveh, and that the airplane was the belly of the whale"[48]. In the next few weeks, Lemuel knew that he was feeling a call from God to try the pastoral position in Philadelphia. They moved in July of 1988.

Love Truth Congregation - 1994

A support group of local Mennonite leaders that included Freeman Miller, Luke Stoltzfus, Ross Bender, and Jim Leaman was developed to help Pastor So for the first two years. After becoming familiar with his new environment for one year, he moved the ministry from the Logan area into rented facilities near Sixth and Chew, an area where more Chinese families were living. None of the attenders of the Logan church transferred to the new area except for Chung Low, an elderly gentleman who became a member after the move. Pastor So called their new congregation the Love Truth Chinese Mennonite Church, a name derived from a Chinese figure of speech which translates as "loving the truth". Initially, they prayed for three couples to begin their fellowship. Their prayer was answered two months later as three couples, bringing a variety of Chinese ethnic backgrounds including Lao, Vietnamese, and Cambodian began attending a Bible Study on August 16, 1989.

One early method of outreach that the So family used in the Chinese community was to teach Chinese to children on Saturday. They began these classes because many Chinese parents felt a desire to have their children learn to read and write in Chinese. They conducted these classes for children 6 to 12 years old and had as many as 110 students. They have done this for nine years and currently have a class of 43.

Another method of contacting new families was through a monthly newsletter, "Good Tidings", which Lemuel wrote and mailed out for about five years. They now distribute the Chinese evangelistic newspaper, "Herald", which many Chinese churches, both Mennonite and others, use in Philadelphia and New York. In addition to his pastoring, Lemuel has also translated several Mennonite documents and books, such as "The

So brothers - Sing Kin and Lemuel So, Pastors at Love Truth Chinese Mennonite Church

Mennonite Confession of Faith" and is currently working on C.J. Dyck's "Introduction to Mennonite History". Also for three years he has edited a quarterly newsletter for the eighteen Chinese Mennonite Churches in North America.

They used the rented church for two and a half years. Lemuel was ordained as pastor on September 17th, 1989. The congregation bought a residential property at 600 Chew Ave. in October 1991. They renovated the property to have a meeting room in the basement with an outside entrance and classrooms on the first and second floors.

The current membership stands at 36 with an average attendance of 65. About 40% come from a Christian background and the other 60% from Buddhist or non-religious backgrounds. Although the worship services were initially led in both the Cantonese and Mandarin languages, the congregation currently holds two different services each Sunday, one in Cantonese and one in English. Once a month a joint service is held. There are frequent movements to or from Hong Kong, or other cities in the United States for work or study. Their church grows by people bringing friends and neighbors to Sunday morning services. Pastor So is currently seeking to have a Sabbatical for study and refreshment. He has invited his brother, Sing Kin So, a pastor in Hong Kong for ten years, to pastor the church during this transition.

Abundant Life Chinese Mennonite Church

Ted Yao had a gift for church-planting. Although he was not the type of leader who would sustain a church in a long-term leadership role, he had a vision for new congregations. This is what led him to begin planting the second church for the Chinese community in Philadelphia – Abundant Life. In 1987 he began with a Bible study group of older persons in a community center near 15th and Moore. He soon asked the Philip Dich family to come and pastor this group.

Yao knew the Dich family from Vietnam where they had lived before coming to the United States. They were residing in northern New Jersey when Yao issued the invitation. Philip Dich had become a Christian in high school in Vietnam. Although he had no Mennonite connections prior to this, he trusted Ted Yao's leadership and connections with the Mennonite church. Philip was employed with the Estee Company and continued working for a while along with his pastoral duties, both at the factory and at a Lutheran social service agency. Shirley had some Bible School training in Taiwan. She was skilled in piano and regularly played for the services. They had five daughters who helped in the ministry a great deal. Philip was licensed as a pastor by the Lancaster Conference in 1988. He was ordained in 1994.

Philip and Shirley Dich Family Irene, Joyce, Esther, Elizabeth, Grace, Philip and Shirley - 1987

Pastor Truong Tu of the Abundant Life Chinese Mennonite Church - 1999

Services were held in their home on South 15th Street until a store-front building was purchased at Broad and Moore in 1991. Philip invited the Truong Tu family, whom they knew from their time in Saigon, to assist in the leadership of the church in 1993. Dorcas Tu says that their first purpose in coming to Philadelphia from the west coast where they had previously been residing was for their two children's education. The Dich girls had gone to Lancaster Mennonite High School, so the Tu children did also.

When Shirley passed away in February of 1994, Philip accepted an assignment as a missionary to Chinese in Eastern Europe. He came and went in about two month intervals. This left the main pastoral responsibility to Truong and Dorcas Tu. The Tu family has been graciously supported by a committed lay ministry team that has included Lily Lee, Quoch Chin Min, Howard Chau, and others in the church. Truong describes the fact that, in Chinese, the word, "pastor", can have two different meanings. The first meaning is that of a "proclaimer", or one who concentrates on evangelistic preaching. The second meaning is more akin to that of a shepherd, or one who stays in one place to minister to the gathered believers. In his role as pastor at Abundant Life, he has taken on more of the latter role.

The church has faced a number of obstacles in its evangelism to Chinese immigrants including language and cultural issues. The congregation works to get around these obstacles by playing an active role in the Chinese immigrant community in South Philadelphia. They offer English classes to new immigrants who are attempting to adjust to American life and help to publish a gospel newspaper written in Chinese called The Herald that concentrates on social topics such as education, medicine, and jobs. Current membership is about 60, and Sunday morning attendance about 70. This fills their meeting room. While most of the adult members are first-generation Chinese refugees, the congregation has developed strong children and youth Sunday School programs and a summer day camp. Worship services are held in both Cantonese and English. Since the fall of 1999, the Abundant Life congregation has been developing their own church plant in South Philadelphia. With the help of Leonard Burkholder, they hold weekly Sunday afternoon services for Indonesian immigrants.

The Philadelphia Cambodian Mennonite Church

In 1989, Ted Yao began yet another Mennonite church that he envisioned being for the Chinese community in Upper Darby on the western edge of Philadelphia. Initially, the service took place on Sunday and was in English. The hymnbooks were written in both English and Chinese.

For various reasons, the church began to attract Cambodians as well as Chinese who had lived most of their lives in Cambodia. Members of the church were bilingual, some speaking both Chinese and Cambodian. A majority of the members did not understand English. Within a year of the founding of the congregation, Pastor Yao resigned as pastor of the church. Bishop Luke and Miriam Stoltzfus led the church for two years, while preparing Sarin Lay (see sidebar) to be the leader.

Language differences sometimes made the pastoral role difficult for Bishop Stoltzfus, but he countered this by asking Vanna Lay, a member of the congregation, to translate his sermons for him. Stoltzfus would write out the sermons a couple of days before Sunday and Lay would translate them into the Cambodian language. Both sermons would then be read on Sunday morning. Lay, at times, would often point out the difficulty in translating "God words" into Cambodian, since the Cambodian language has several words for God.

Sarin Lay and his family had become acquainted with the Mennonite Church when they had been invited by Paul Kao, a church lay member, to attend the Chinese Mennonite Church in Upper Darby.

Ted Yao baptising Sopal - Ted Yao, Sopal, Ben Yao - 1990

Sarin Lay: From Buddhist Monk to Mennonite Pastor

As the Lay family were fleeing from the "killing fields" of Cambodia, Sarin, who had been a Buddhist monk, had a vision of a man in white, who told him to follow Him over the mountains. Soon after, Sarin found a crumpled piece of **Pastor Sarin Lay of Philadelphia Cambodian Mennonite Church - 1999** *paper on a village street when he went to buy food. The picture on the front of the tract was the same man he had seen in his dream. When they reached the Thai border, they learned about Jesus in the refugee camp. He received Jesus as his Savior and began studying the Word and witnessing to others.*

Sarin had experience as a church planter when he was a refugee in Thailand, Philippines, and Harrisburg, Pennsylvania. The church experienced a rapid rise in membership during the two years as Lay continually brought forth new families to come to the church. Bishop Stoltzfus baptized over 100 new members in one year.

Pastor Lay was licensed by the Lancaster Conference in 1992. The congregation is today the fastest-growing Mennonite church in the city. The membership has grown to 200. Deacons were chosen, talented musicians offered their help in the services, and people began to call for a building of their own.

Through the prayers and support of the membership, a building was found in

Baptismal Class at Cambodian M.C. - 1991
Leadership in first two rows: Miriam and Luke Stoltzfus, Sarin and Hun Lay, Savonny Prak, Soth Mar, Vanna Lay, Paul Kao

1993. It was just two blocks from the rented church building at 711 Snyder Avenue. They were amazed what God did when they asked, inspired by Matthew 7:7: "Ask, and you will receive".

During the negotiation and bidding for the new building, God sent the Leonard Burkholder Family to help the congregation Burkholder worked as Eastern Mennonite Mission's fieldworker for foreign-language church plants. Together with Pastor Sarin Lay, he led a small group of volunteers to fix up the new building. The first services were held in the new church building in January 1994. Renovations continue as time and materials are available. An average of 60 or 70 members attend each Sunday with a total membership of almost 200 members.

Christian Life Mennonite Church

The history of the Christian Life Mennonite Church in Philadelphia is the story of transition, but with the outcome of a jubilant congregation with a strong family environment. In 1990, Pastor Parker Mavi, a South African native, planted a church with the help of Bishop Stoltzfus. The purpose of this new congregation was to locate itself in the African-American middle-class neighborhood of Mt. Airy, since most mission churches reached out to primarily low-income city dwellers. By doing so, Pastor Mavi and Bishop Stoltzfus hoped to attract a different type of congregant than the Philadelphia Mennonite Church had been used to up until this point.

Although the congregation did not fill the pews in the way that they had initially envisioned, it did fairly quickly begin to attract a diversity of other church participants. Between 1993 and 1994, a typical Sunday morning service would consist of African-American community members, traditional white Mennonites, a Palestinian couple, African families, and Temple University students. By this time, Pastor Mavi had moved on to take a position with the Salvation Army, and the leadership of the congregation consisted of a team ministry. Pastors James Dennis, Phil Stauffer and Joe Franczyk divided up the pastoral responsibilities between themselves. Dennis, a construction worker, was African-American. Franczyk, a social worker, and Stauffer, a thrift-store manager, were both white. February 14, 1993 Congregational Meeting minutes noted that, "the style change may be painful; change from one leader to a leadership team".

Parker and Ana Mavi - 1990

In 1995, it was decided that the team ministry approach was not working as well as originally hoped, and that one of the three team members should be chosen as the sole minister for the congregation. A vote was taken and James Dennis was elected. Drawing on his unique background (see sidebar) and a dedicated spirit of ministry, Pastor Dennis was ordained on December 3, 1995 and continues to lead the congregation today which consists primarily of African-American families, some of whom have been in the church since its inception. Georgette Harris and Marie and Harvey Davis both date their membership back to the days of Pastor Mavi. Georgette mentions that the "fact that we are still together as a thriving congregation is truly a testimony to God" and notes that Pastor Dennis has been crucial in holding them together. "Pastor Dennis preaches the Bible truth!" she says. Services are lively and reception of visitors is warm.

Christian Life Mennonite Church has renewed its mission of outreach to their surrounding community. A food bank that also gives out used clothing to the needy was begun by the church and is directed today by Deaconness Brenda Cherry. On September 10, 1995, a new van was purchased by the church for community outreach efforts. Pastor Dennis drives people to church every Sunday for church services. Many of the people who now attend Christian Life live not in Mt. Airy, but in Dennis' neighborhood in North Philadelphia.

James Dennis:
Preaching the Bible Truth

The following auto-biographical story was extracted from a longer article written by James Dennis, pastor of Christian Life Mennonite Church. The article was published in the Missionary Messenger, February 1989.

James and Kathleen Dennis
1999

"I grew up with a lot of hurt and resentment. I am here today because of the saving power and the grace of our Lord and Savior Jesus Christ. I came from a small town in southeastern Georgia. My father was an alcoholic, but in spite of his alcoholism I knew he loved me. When I was four years old, my mother and father were separated. My youngest sister and I stayed with my father. We grew up in a poverty-stricken neighborhood, where there was a lot of racism. My hurt turned to anger and hatred...I had started drinking at the age of 16, and in addition to that, I was carrying a gun...This condition, combined with my hurt, resentment, and hatred, meant trouble. Every time I got into trouble, my father would come to my rescue. He warned me the day would come when he would not be able to help me. Finally it happened as he predicted, and at the age of 19 I was sent to the chain gang. My father came to see me, but they would not allow him to get me out. Trying to be big, bad, and bold, as if being locked up didn't mean anything, I told my father I would be all right. Eventually he was able to get me out of the chain gang, and the authorities told me that if I would go into the military service, they would erase this from my record.

"Several years later I volunteered for the draft. I joined the army on January 25, 1968, and was sent to Vietnam in June 1968. But I went AWOL and didn't arrive in Vietnam until late July. In Vietnam I became a black militant leader. I was known to be a good fighter, and some of the fellows even called me a bit crazy. I formed a group of black militants who were against all whites. Early in my life I had made a vow that I would one day kill a white man. Growing up in the midst of so much racism and hatred, seeing all those signs setting boundaries between blacks and whites, I vowed that I was going to kill me a white man if it were the last thing I do...Thirteen days before I was to leave Vietnam I was hit by a mine explosion... I returned to the United States as violent and angry as I had left it, still fighting people, especially whites...Deep within my heart I still carried the intent to kill a white man. I lived in Germantown in a neighborhood that was partly black and partly white. I was so militant against whites that I even disliked the children. When the little white children would ask to play with my children, I would not permit it..."

After a few subsequent violent incidents, James ended up in prison. Through a relationship with another inmate, Herbert, James became a Christian and, after his release, found his way to Diamond Street Mennonite Church. At Diamond Street, James found a community of support who eventually gave him leadership in the congregation, steering him toward the pastoral role that he now holds at Christian Life Church.

"I can relate to the dream of Martin Luther King that one day all people - black, white, brown, yellow, red - will walk hand in hand. Today I can walk hand in hand with my brothers and sisters, whatever their color, because God has given me a love that come from Him. He is the source of all the love we will ever need to be the people he wants us to be."

Ethiopian Evangelical Fellowship

Ethiopian Evangelical Fellowship grew out of the witness of a West Philadelphia Mennonite Fellowship member, Yeshitela Mengistu. Mengistu was a pastor in the Mennonite-affiliated Meserete Kristos (Christ Foundation) Church of Ethiopia. He came for graduate study at Associated Mennonite Biblical Seminaries, and later for a degree in Economic Development at Eastern College in St. Davids, Pennsylvania.

While at Eastern, Mengistu learned that the city's Ethiopian population of 2,500 lacked an evangelical Christian church. In 1990 he began holding Amharic language services in a Presbyterian church building not far from West Philadelphia Mennonite Fellowship. He received personal and administrative support from Philadelphia District Bishop Luke Stoltzfus, and some financial support from Eastern Mennonite Missions.

Mengistu noted that many Ethiopians in America are driven to workaholism and regard church attendance as a waste of time. Tribal factionalism is another challenge to Ethiopian church development. Now only Amharic, the national language, is used because Mengistu wanted people to see that Jesus Christ is Lord over tribes and government.

Yeshetile Mengistu Family and friends from Ethiopia - Solomon and Lydia Kebede, son of Yeshetila, Abebetch wife of Yeshetila, Meba (daughter of Yeshetila) Yeshetila and Kedu Delchume - 1994

There was a growing concern of the welfare of Ethiopians in the Philadelphia area in the latter part of the 1980s. This concern was particularly spurred by the death of two people who committed suicide and two others who were in hospitals because of mental depression. Although there was an Ethiopian fellowship in the suburbs that had begun some years before, the need to begin such a fellowship in the Philadelphia area was clearly evident. A fellowship began for a brief period of time, but later was disbanded for various reasons. There continued to be a growing need for a Christian fellowship in the Philadelphia community. This need was the catalyst which gave birth to the Ethiopian Evangelical Church in Philadelphia (EECP) in 1990.

Pastor Yeshitela Mengistu began his ministry in West Philadelphia with a handful of believers who were committed to preaching the gospel of Jesus Christ to the Ethiopian community.

The main objectives of this new ministry were to evangelize, fellowship, and help Ethiopians assimilate into the American culture. A number of individuals experienced life-changing moments through the church. Word of these changes began to spread throughout the Ethiopian community, spurring the growth of the church. Bible study groups formed and were held in the homes of some church members. A weekly prayer program was also started. A choir consisting of six individuals using an electronic synthesizer led the congregation in worship. In order to strengthen unity among the group, annual picnics were instituted as a means to bringing church members together to enjoy outdoor fun, barbecue and fellowship.

Nigist and Pastor Tesfaye Setargie - 1999

Mengistu worked as a church planter under EMM and so related to the Lancaster Conference. He traveled in the United States and Canada to visit Ethiopian congregations. This led him to leave Philadelphia to plant a church in St. Louis in 1994. For a period of approximately three years, EECP did not have a pastor. During this time, all of the church's spiritual and administrative needs were carried out by the Elders committee. All of the programs that were previously in place continued without interruption. However, the church continued to search for a pastor. In the fall of 1997, Pastor Tesfaye Setargie, along with his wife, Nigist, and two children, moved to the Philadelphia area so that Tesfaye could serve as lead pastor at the church.

The church continued its ministry to the Ethiopian community in the same manner as in previous years. Yearly conferences and seminars challenged people to strengthen their Christian faith and transform their lives. In August of 1999, EECP moved its worship location to Upper Darby just outside the city, strategically positioning itself in the concentration of Ethiopians in the areas of West Philadelphia and the western suburbs. This also facilitated the holding of all the church programs such as weekly prayer meetings, all-night prayer meetings and Sunday worship in one church facility. The first annual camp retreat, held in 1999 for three days, fostered the development of relationships among church members.

The congregation currently serves approximately thirty members. Teshome Gebremedhin, one of the elders at EECP, describes the leadership's vision for the congregation: "EECP continues to lift up its hands in submission to God who by His awesome power sustains and guides it so that this church will be a lighthouse to the Ethiopian community in the Philadelphia area".

New Mercies Mennonite Church

In 1992, Reverends Charles Bulford and Nadine Smith-Bulford were serving as associate ministers at Faith Chapel Church of God in Christ. One night they found themselves both lying awake in the middle of the night, each separately hearing a calling from God to plant a church. Furthermore, they both knew that the church was to be located in the East Falls area of Philadelphia and that its name was to be New Mercies Church. They agreed in prayer with each other and then with their pastor, Bishop Eugene H. Graves, Jr., that God was calling them to this transition in their lives. After continued prayer with the Presiding Bishop, Bishop O.T. Jones, Jr., the Bulfords were sent by him as "missionaries to the Mennonites". They received permission to approach the Mennonites about planting a church in Philadelphia.

Why Mennonites? Nadine and Charles describe a "Macedonian call" that they received from the Mennonite Church. Charles had some prior connections with the Mennonite church in Northeast Pennsylvania and in Philadelphia at West Philadelphia Mennonite Fellowship. The pastoral couple spent time talking with Bishop

Leadership at New Mercies Mennonite Church - 1998
Charles and Nadine (Smith) Bulford with Robert George

Freeman Miller, former Bishop Luke Stoltzfus, and Lindsey Robinson in their discernment process and felt that the Mennonite church was an appropriate vehicle for starting their new church. Both Franconia and Lancaster Conferences invited them to work with them, but the pastoral couple felt a calling to join Lancaster Conference.

On January 1, 1993, the Home Ministries Department of Eastern Mennonite Missions of the Lancaster Conference approved their plan for a new church to be planted in the East Falls neighborhood of Philadelphia. Sunday, February 14, 1993, Faith Chapel Church of God in Christ laid hands on the Bulfords and sent them to their new work. In March, at the Spring Assembly of the Lancaster Conference, the Bulfords were officially commissioned to plant New Mercies Mennonite Church. As part of the Philadelphia District under Bishop Luke Stoltzfus, New Mercies Mennonite Church began with a membership of three, the pastors and their daughter Rachel, the self-described Junior Pastor of New Mercies.

The church held its first prayer-care cell meeting (Bible Study) in September of 1993 at the pastor's home, 1826 North Bouvier Street in North Philadelphia. The Bulfords moved into the East Falls neighborhood in October of 1993. In December of 1993, New Mercies began to hold worship services in the pastors' new home at 3015 Midvale Avenue in the East Falls area of the city, a very underchurched community. Charles estimates that of the 20,000 residents of the East Falls community, less than 1000 attend church[49]. Combining an evangelical fervor with a sociological analysis of their community, the Bulfords continued the process of establishing relationships with families in the neighborhood. "East Falls has 20,000 people and a combined Protestant church attendance of 200. It has the very rich, the very poor, and the in-betweens. We think God has led us here because East Falls is ripe for the gospel," Charles concludes. Other churches were skeptical about a Mennonite church in the community. Every church but the Catholic church thought that they would leave within a short time.

When the Bulfords first arrived in East Falls, they took an unusual first step for church planters and went straight to the fire department. "The fire captain may be the most strategic person for an urban evangelist to get to know", says Charles. The Bulfords volunteered to assist the department in handing out smoke detectors door to door. Doing so proved to be a good way to meet a large number of people in the neighborhood. As they would introduce themselves, they would also spread the word about the new congregation. The next year they returned to most of these same houses armed with health information from the fire department, showing people in the community that they were a presence in the neighborhood.

As the New Mercies core group began to grow, the East Falls community experienced racial unrest during the spring and summer of 1994. The Bulfords were personally exposed to much hostility and one person was injured while leaving their home during this time of trouble. New Mercies became a very visible church as it worked with others for reconciliation. In September, this led to a decision by the Evangelical Lutheran Church of the Redeemer, located at 3642 Midvale Avenue at Conrad Street, to rent their worship facility to New Mercies.

In March of 1995, New Mercies held its first baptism. Nine were baptized including three generations of the Smith-Carter family. During 1995, the church established its Constitution and By-Laws and named the Board of Servants to be its governing unit. Three were baptized in February of 1996. At the 1996 Spring Assembly, New Mercies Mennonite Church was declared to be an established, self-sustaining church by the Lancaster Conference.

On April 26, 1998, fifteen persons were baptized. New Mercies has a membership of about 65 (including children). On a typical Sunday morning, visitors will find a multi-racial group of church participants, celebrating God in a joyous fashion through an abundance of singing and energetic sermons delivered by either Pastor Nadine or Pastor Charles. The congregation now meets in the Falls Presbyterian Church at Vaux and Midvale Streets. According to Pastor Charles, their aim is to become a "kingdom congregation, not multi-class or multi-cultural, but instead King-centered, a place where people live in rightness with each other regardless of the dividing issues".

Salam Mennonite Fellowship

Palestinian Christians George and Frosina Kuttab are doing something they've wanted to do for more than twenty years - start a church for Arabic-speaking people in the United States. It doesn't seem to matter that they're both in their 70s.

Both grew up in the deeply religious Greek Orthodox community in Palestine. After a personal commitment to Jesus, George attended a Nazarene Bible college to prepare for Christian ministry. George and his mother (who was warned in a dream) made a decision to leave Jerusalem and move to Jordan two days before the nation of Israel declared its independence and the Arab quarter of Jerusalem (their old home) was bombed.

During the six years that George worked in Zerka, Jordan, he met Frosina. She became a committed Christian and was baptized in an Assemblies of God Church. Her pastor offered to send Frosina to Nazareth for nurses training. After four years of study, she returned home to Jordan, part of the last group to get out of the country before Israeli forces closed the border. George and Frosina married in 1951 and worked in the Zerka Church until 1954, when they asked for a transfer back to George's home area near Jerusalem.

Pastor George and Frosena Kuttab - 1998

Their dreams of raising a family and working in nursing and Christian ministry in the Palestinian Arab community were complicated by countless political upheavals and uncertainties. Shortly after the Six Day War in 1967 when Israel occupied the Gaza Strip and the West Bank, Frosina and her youngest child traveled to visit friends and family in Jordan. The Israelis had repeatedly announced that the border would be open for two weeks. But once there, she and thousands of other Palestinians, were denied reentry visas into Israel. The border was sealed. Determined to rejoin George and her five children, Frosina waded across the Jordan River and walked through the mountains carrying her nursing baby, Grace.

In 1970, the Kuttab family came to the United States so that their children could go to school at Messiah College. It was not easy for a family of nine to survive without an income. Although George was an experienced pastor, it was not easy for him to find a pastoral position in the United States and the Arab community in Pennsylvania was not large enough to support him with a church building or members. He finally decided to work temporarily for a publishing house in New Jersey while beginning a fellowship among Arabic-speaking people in Jersey City, New Jersey and in New York. After retiring from the publishing house, he filled interim pastorates at West Chester Mennonite Church in Pennsylvania and Northside Mennonite Church in Lima, Ohio.

When they moved back to Philadelphia in 1989, Pastor Kuttab was officially licensed as a minister by the Lancaster Conference. He continued his work among Arabic-speaking people and eventually started a cell group in a home in Philadelphia in 1996. This was the beginning of the Salam Mennonite Fellowship. The group has grown to 20 to 30 adults and children. They would like to locate in an area of the city where more Arabic-speaking people live.

Kapatiran Christian Church

Ton and Pollie Alcantara came to the United States in March 1991, eight months after they got married, to pursue graduate studies at Eastern College. In February 1992 they, together with two other friends initiated a monthly fellowship among Filipino-Americans in the area, which they called "Kapit-Bisig (linking arms) Christian Fellowship". This fellowship met monthly for encouragement, prayer, singing, sharing Philippine news and eating meals together. By 1993, Ton finished his graduate studies and proceeded to do theological studies at Eastern Baptist Theological Seminary. That same year the couple started two small Bible study groups (one in Northeast Philadelphia and one in Norristown) to meet the needs of the Fellowship's Filipino-American constituents for deeper knowledge of God's word. In 1994 another Bible study group was organized among computer programmers. Many of the recent area Filipinos had come to the U.S. to fill the need in the computer industry in the 1990's.

Pastor Ton and Pollie Alcantara - 1998

The idea of a Filipino evangelical church emerged from the Northeast Philadelphia group out of a desire to freely express and exercise their faith in Christ, given their own distinct culture. This group challenged Pastor Alcantara to lead the church planting effort. In June 1995, after his graduation from Seminary, and after prayerful consideration, he accepted the challenge. He explored a number of denominations for possible affiliation, and finally decided to join the Mennonite Church, having been influenced by his professor, Ron Sider, at seminary.

The Kapatiran Congregation at the new building - 1998

Church planting efforts officially began in September 1995 when Pastor Alcantara entered into an agreement with Eastern Mennonite Missions' Home Ministries. Shortly after that, he invited six Filipino evangelicals, mostly from bible study groups, to form the church planting team. Its task was to perform key roles in the church planting venture, which include, praying, formulating the church biblical framework, strategic planning, providing collective leadership, and preparing for the first public worship celebration. They named the church "Kapitaran Christian Church", or KCC for short. "Kapatiran" is a gender-neutral Tagalog term for brotherhood/sisterhood.

Finally, on May 5, 1996, the first public worship was celebrated at the Fellowship Hall of the Presbyterian Church of the Covenant in Bala Cynwyd, Pennsylvania. The congregation rented this place for their Sunday afternoon worship celebration for the next two and a half years. They started with an average attendance of 25 adults and 6 children.

Why another church in the metropolitan area where there is mushroom of churches? Pastor Alcantara says that most Filipinos are Roman Catholics and there is very little outreach done among this ethnic group in Philadelphia. The official migration of Filipinos to the United States dates back to the turn of the century when the U.S. colonized the Philippines in 1898. According to the 1990 census; there are about 7,000 Filipinos in Greater Philadelphia and might reach to around 10,000 by the year 2000.

Just like other foreign immigrants, Filipinos come to America for various reasons, foremost of which is economic - the pursuit of the "American Dream", or better opportunities than what they left behind in the Philippines. The challenge for KCC is to walk with the Filipino migrants in their process of integration to the mainstream of American society, assist them in their struggles, rejoice with them in their successes, and empathize with them in their frustrations.

In October 1998, the congregation purchased a new church building. Although this came earlier than they had planned, the new building provides extra space and freedom for the congregation to fulfill their mission. The move to the new building was made on the first week of November with an inaugural service held on the first Sunday. Pastor Alcantara says that, "The year 1998 proved to be a harvest year, after a long time of planting the seed of the gospel. The church's membership doubled and average attendance rose to 65 (including children). A lot of new Bible study groups were organized making a total of 12 groups. New ministry groups and teams were also formed such as the Philadelphia team; couples, singles, women's and youth groups. The worship team was also strengthened as God brought a number of gifted musicians into the congregation.

Way of Life Ministries

In 1993 when they first sensed the call to plant a church, Dwayne and Pam were both actively involved in ministry in the United Methodist Church. In 1996, while still involved with the Methodists, they began a more intense exploration of God's call to plant a new ministry. Following numerous and intense hours of midnight prayer, they conducted prayer "drives" and prayer "walks" in various communities throughout the West Philadelphia area, mapping the areas as they went along. Soon they realized that they were being drawn to a particular target ministry area (the Mantua/Millcreek community) and a particular section of vacant lots along 44th Street between Haverford and Fairmount Avenues.

After repeated midnight prayer, drives and walks, they began to pen what they believed they were hearing from God. They began to write the vision and mission of this new ministry applying Ephesians 2:8-10 as the foundational scripture and following with an action plan for wholistic ministry. The name of the ministry was taken from the latter part of the 10th verse (NRSV), "way of life". The focus of this new ministry was to reconcile persons to one another and to God by addressing spiritual, social, physical, financial and mental and emotional concerns.

Pastors Dwayne and Pam Royster
1999

In May 1997 the Roysters opened their home to interested persons including close family and friends, for an initial time of visioning, discernment and sharing to "hear what the Spirit was saying". This initial gathering soon developed into a series of weekly prayer and bible study sessions for adults and children (approximately seven families) based on the vision and mission that God had given them for the new ministry. In June 1997, both Dwayne and Pam left their former work with the United Methodist Church to plant a new ministry called, "Way of Life Ministries".

It was decided that Way of Life Ministries would be a Philadelphia District church plant as opposed to being strictly an EMM church plant. This had not yet been done in the recent history of the District. During the first year Philadelphia District leadership and Home Ministries staff worked to devise a plan for this proposed "new model" of partnership between the District and Home Ministries. Bishop Miller, Charles Bulford, Philadelphia EMM representative, Mervin Charles, Home Ministries Director, and Henry Buckwalter, Associate Director were instrumental in formulating the groundwork for this new model of partnership.

Meanwhile, the weekly prayer and bible study sessions continued throughout the Fall of 1997 until the first worship service was held on Sunday, December 7, 1997 in the living and dining room of the Royster home. At the end of January 1998 it was decided that the worship services and Bible studies should be held in a location closer to the target community and ministry area. In February 1998, Way of Life Ministries relocated to the Millcreek Arts and Cultural Center at 4624 Lancaster Avenue.

Finally, in June 1998 the partnership plan between the Philadelphia District and Home Ministries was completed and both entities began to support Way of Life Ministries. In September 1998, Dwayne was ordained and Pam was commissioned by the Lancaster Conference of the Mennonite church to serve as a church planting team in the Philadelphia District.

At the end of October 1998, the City of Philadelphia contacted the pastors about the possibility of going to settlement on the vacant lots at 44th Street between Haverford and Fairmount Avenues. There were only a few days before the final deadline, and, because this was a new ministry, funds were very limited. Nonetheless, in November 1998, God miraculously enabled the church to purchase those vacant lots through a church planting grant by the Eastern District of the General Conference Mennonite Church. The grant money had been set aside many years earlier for a church planting effort in Eastern District that did not materialize. All parties were astonished that the size of the grant was almost the exact dollar amount needed for settlement on the land! Way of Life Ministries hopes to someday build a permanent worship facility on this land that God has provided. On Sunday, December 6, 1998, Way of Life Ministries celebrated its first church anniversary with the theme, "We've Come This Far by Faith", and ended the year with the birth of its still thriving Matthew 25 Outreach

Ministry to the homeless, and a rapidly growing children and youth ministry.

The early part of 1999 was a turbulent time for the pastors and the entire congregation. While the pastors/church planters took a leave of absence to strengthen their ministry and marriage, Rev. Emmanuel Itapson, seminary intern, served as the interim pastor under the guidance of the Bishop Freeman Miller, Philadelphia District. By most standards, this ministry should have folded, but God saw fit to keep this church family together. The God-given vision and mission was being lived out in full operation amongst the entire local Body. As a result, the pastors/church planters returned to leadership in the latter part of 1999, and the church family continued to grow in faith and in faces.

On Sunday, October 3, 1999 the Way of Life church family had a wonderful "new beginning". The church experienced a powerful "move of God" during the first worship service in its newly leased worship facility at 4500 Westminster Avenue, still in the heart of the target ministry area. On Sunday, December 5, 1999, the church will celebrate its 2nd church anniversary. Pastors Dwayne and Pam say that, "...with the new worship location, new members and attenders, renewed minds, renewed hearts, and a renewed commitment and fervor for serving God in excellence, the Way of Life Ministries truly thanks God for His grace to start again!"

Philadelphia Mennonite High School:
A Dream Whose Time Had Come
-by Arbutus Sider

On September 3, 1998 fifty-three 9th, 10th and 11th grade students entered the doors of Philadelphia Mennonite High School, proud pioneers in a brand new school. A dream, in the planning since 1993, had finally come true. A dream of an urban Mennonite high school to train youth with high quality education within an Anabaptist Christian context. A dream of a culturally diverse community, enabling students to achieve their full potential and to develop a lifestyle of service and peacemaking.

It is striking and encouraging to see how many of the elements of the present Philadelphia Mennonite High School Mission Statement were already in the minds of the Feasibility Task Force members, Leonard Burkholder, Philip Dich, James Leaman and Rosalie Rolon Dow when they recommended to the Philadelphia Mennonite pastors "that a Mennonite secondary school be planted in Philadelphia". The date was August 11, 1994. The Task Force summarized their work and vision with these words:

> There is deep concern for training our youth with high quality education within an Anabaptist Christian context. We value the cultural diversity within the Philadelphia Mennonite community and believe this school can enhance the spirit of reconciliation and peacemaking. Our youth need to be trained to be contributing members and leaders in the church and community. A Mennonite secondary school in Philadelphia will help fulfill this vision.

In October, 1994, the Task Force began the process of forming a Board of Directors for the school. The following individuals did serve at some time or other on the board of Philadelphia

Miriam and Luke Stoltzfus' 50th Wedding Anniversary with Ron and Arbutus Sider - 1998

Mennonite High School: Nadine Smith Bulford, Leonard Dow, Tim Martin Johnson, Peter Khuu, Juan Naranjo, Calenthia Dowdy, Efrain Cotto, and Arbutus Sider. With the addition of task force members, Leonard Burkholder, Rosalie Rolon Dow and Jim Leaman, and with the ever-present support of Bishop Luke and Miriam Stoltzfus and Bishop Freeman Miller, they formed the core of the start-up board of the new high school. Arbutus Sider, from New Mercies Mennonite Church, was assigned to be Board Chair, and Lily Lee, of Abundant Life Chinese Mennonite Church, took on the role of Co-Chair. Jim Leaman especially filled numerous roles in the early years as pastor of Oxford Circle Mennonite Church, early dreamer, leader of the Feasibility Study, first Board Chair, first staff person as Coordinator of Development and Public Relations, first UPDATE! newsletter editor, etc., etc..

Early one mid-October morning Ilya Johnson, a youth leader at Diamond Street Mennonite Church, found out through a neighbor that a three-story school building on a quiet street in the downtown Art Museum area was for sale. Ilya notified the Board and we were quickly ready for action. We voted unanimously to accept the recommendation of the Executive Board to enter into negotiations with the Ukrainian Catholic Archdiocese for purchase of the St. Nicholas School building.

Barbara Moses was not our first candidate interviewed, and the decision to hire her did not come easily. She had been "discovered" by Polly Ann Brown during a "chance" meeting at the University of Pennsylvania when Polly Ann was teaching there. We believe, in fact, that it was God who brought her to us "for such a time as this." The Search Committee listened to her vision for the school and the fit seemed near perfect. An experienced urban educator; a woman of color; an educational philosophy that paralleled our own. And yet, the committee wrestled long and hard with the question of whether a non-Mennonite principal-Barbara Moses is a Baptist- was a wise choice for the beginning years of a new Mennonite high school. Eventually, the Board decided that Barbara Moses was indeed the person for the job. Her commitment to God and to the church family she grew up in was strong. We discovered, too, that she is very much in agreement with Anabaptist beliefs. Equally important, she was willing to be affiliated with the Mennonite church. Bishop Freeman Miller offered to take on the responsibility of introducing Barbara Moses to the Anabaptist perspective, and to the Mennonite community in and beyond Philadelphia. On December 22, 1997 the Board of Philadelphia Mennonite High School voted to hire Barbara Moses as the first principal of the school.

Philadelphia Mennonite High School - 1998

Mid-January Deanna Slamans, a Messiah Graduate of 1995, was hired as a full time Administrative Assistant. At the end of January Dan Ceglia was hired on a part time basis to coordinate the renovation of the building. However, a few months later it became clear that much more than building renovations needed coordination. Dan Ceglia stepped into the breach; by the end of April he was functioning as a full time Project Manager, coordinating the work of the total staff.

May, June and early July of '98 were weeks during which Barbara Moses and Polly Ann Brown interviewed and hired four full time teachers: Randy Nyce, Keena Thrush, Marlene Brubaker and Kelly Thrush. One additional full time person, receptionist Maria Montanez, added her pleasant smile to the front office staff at the beginning of September as a Mennonite Central Committee worker.

Now the only faces missing were those of the students. Throughout the summer of '98, staff and board became increasingly anxious since there were few early applicants. Our spring efforts at

Student Body with Faculty in 1998 - 99 term

"getting the word out" included three Open Houses in March and April. Those who attended went away highly enthused, but the number who came was disappointingly low considering the five hundred piece mailing that had been sent out, together with follow-up phone calls. Nor did much student support come from the Mennonite churches in the city. By July 20 we had only twelve students enrolled. By August 19 that number had more than doubled, and by the middle of September, doubled again. In the end it was the free advertising of generous media coverage-two major newspaper stories and three TV stations with positive news clips that brought a flurry of requests for applications. By the middle of September we had fifty-three students, just eight short of our goal of sixty!

On the opening day of school, September 3, 1998, students and staff shared a brief worship time with some twelve to fifteen Mennonite church leaders attending the monthly Philadelphia Anabaptist Network Prayer Breakfast under the leadership of Bishop Freeman Miller. It was a celebrative beginning. Although not all classrooms had yet been fully equipped, the attractively filled bulletin boards, brightly painted walls and newly carpeted floors all contributed to a sense of pride and anticipation.

Students willingly gave their first impressions during the first few weeks of school. What did they like? "It's a new school." "Here, everyone belongs." "There are better, smaller classes; I'll have better communication with my teachers." "These teachers actually teach!" "At my old school all that mattered was that I showed up. I wasn't learning anything." Philadelphia Mennonite High School fills a need as one of very few Protestant high schools in the city. But beyond that it is on the cutting edge of education in a number of ways. Its self-definition as "a culturally diverse community of learners," emphasizes its intent to be multi-cultural at every level, to present learning from many cultural perspectives, and to learn in a communal, interactive way.

The Future of the Mennonite Church in Philadelphia
- by Freeman Miller - July, 1999

It is hazardous to guess the future of the Mennonite Church in this historic city. For if we have a truly unique phenomenon here – 22 urban Anabaptist congregations comprised of eleven language groups – there is no precedent on which to base our conjecture. If it is true that no other group of Mennonite churches anywhere (not to mention in a large city) ever existed with this kind of dynamic diversity, who can begin to imagine what the future might hold? We could be headed for extinction, discovering that this kind of multi-faceted community cannot hold together in the long run. Then again, God may be up to something new in the world-wide church, the beginnings of which we only glimpse here and now. Given the realities of human nature in human community, coupled with the mysterious workings of God's grace in human history, something in between these two "extremes" is more likely. After all, every Christian community is always only one generation from extinction or one generation from rebirth, depending on the holy combination of divine grace and human response.

Bishop Freeman Miller Family - 1999 - Hector, Freeman, Ron, Bryan, Gwen, Naomi, Kai, Janelle, Rhonda

If the newer churches in the city – especially those made up of mostly first-generation immigrants – buy deeply into the American Dream, we can guess that there will be a strong temptation to sell out to materialism and individualism, with the concomitant flight to the suburbs – imitating the white flight of earlier generations and the current exodus of middle-class African Americans. On the other hand, if these same "new Americans" can hold on to the holistic Anabaptist/New Testament view of the church as the counter-culture body of Christ, incarnationally seeking the shalom of the cities to which God has scattered them (reminiscent of Jeremiah 29), we may be on the threshold of a new day as the Mennonite Church marches into a new millennium.

A quick glance at the dramatic changes in the Philadelphia Mennonite church-scape over the past few decades reveals several pertinent "facts." Perhaps the most striking is the simple realization that no single individual got up one morning and decided it was time to plant more language churches in the city. While various Home Ministries (EMM) directors emphasized urban ministries and urban church planting in various forms, most of the "language" churches developed from "natural" linkages as people arrived on our shores. Bishop Luke Stoltzfus actively encouraged the various language churches as they emerged, but in most cases they had begun emerging before the encouragement. After Ted Yao moved to Philadelphia for work reasons, he began organizing Bible studies for Chinese people and these developed into churches. And while EMM and the Philadelphia District invited Lemuel So to come to the city to pastor the new Love Truth Chinese Mennonite Church, that in no way accounts for the fact that Lemuel had received a vision from God earlier, specifically putting Philadelphia on his heart. Recently Emmanuel Itapson left the large ECWA church he was pastoring in Jos, Nigeria, to come to Eastern Baptist Seminary to study. After serving on the pastoral team of Way of Life Ministries (a new Mennonite church plant in West Philadelphia) as a seminary intern, he invited Rev. Victor Musa, President of ECWA to visit Philadelphia. Soon there was discussion about the Mennonites and ECWA teaming up to begin a new ECWA-Mennonite church for Nigerians or Africans in the city. Who knows if this idea will take root?

And so the Kingdom net continues to spread.

As long as current churches are faithful in developing mature disciples for Jesus Christ, it is quite evident that more and more Anabaptist-minded believers will begin finding each other across all kinds of national, ethnic, economic, and geographic lines. This is, after all, what God is up to around the globe. (See Ephesians 1:9-10, where God's purpose is to eventually bring all things in heaven and on earth together under the lordship of Jesus Christ.) In the year 2000 for the first time in human history over half the world's population now lives in cities. "Making disciples of all nations" means making disciples in the cities – to which the nations are streaming. Overseas Mission and Home Mission now combine into Urban Mission. What is happening in Philadelphia is happening and will happen in many other cities. Unless we give up the fight to win the cities for Jesus Christ, the future begins here and it begins now. We cannot retreat to the idyllic rural or small town mentality of the "quiet in the land" simply tilling the soil in peace and quiet, undisturbed by the teeming throngs of the cities. God has "many people in this city," and they reflect the nations, tongues, and tribes that will dance around God's throne in Rev. 2, 9, and 22. We need to begin exercising our "city-zenship" of the New Jerusalem in Old Philadelphia. If we do, we will discover the incredible power of a gospel that combines all who name Jesus as Lord in a dynamic new community of shalom. Entire cities can once again be "turned upside down" as in the book of Acts – the same Holy Spirit is still at work.

I see in my mind's eye a future mosaic of Mennonites covering the city in a "patchwork quilt" or "urban people garden" made up of neighborhood churches where people from every conceivable background come to faith in Jesus as Lord. While first-generation believers might be most comfortable worshiping him in their mother tongue, second and third generations will become more American, speak more English, eat American foods, and intermarry. Surely by now we Mennonites have learned that clinging to the German language and Pennsylvania Dutch traditions are not the best ways to preserve a vital faith in the New World. While the best of each culture's heritage should be carefully taught and preserved as gifts from God, realism and Anabaptist theology tell us that we are all one in Christ and must act like it or become hypocrites to our children and our neighbors. As we help second and third generation Mennonites find each other through education, mission, and fellowship activities (already happening in the monthly Anabaptist leaders prayer breakfasts, the new Philadelphia Mennonite High School, combined seminary courses and seminars, picnics and fellowships), surely a network of interdependent congregations and organizations will emerge for mutual aid and edification, as well as a united witness across the city.

Perhaps some day many smaller churches will network with several "anchor" churches to create mission, service, and hospitality centers, culminating in a downtown (neutral-turf) worship, hotel, retail, and service complex. Not only would such facilities provide jobs and revenue for the Anabaptist network of churches, but also needed services to city residents and the thousands of tourists and international visitors coming to Philadelphia each year. Imagine being told by cab drivers and travel agents to "go to the Mennonite Center while in town; you will receive service second to none 'in the name of Christ.'" What witness that could be! What if the justice system would refer offenders to the historic peace churches who had developed a superior peacemaking and peacekeeping network in formerly violent urban contexts? Can we imagine a future time when people might be told, "If you join the Mennonites, they will either help you find a job or create one for you; but first you must be completely serious about giving yourself 100% to Jesus Christ!"

Anabaptist theology has the answers to contemporary urban ills! We simply need to take our "light from under the bushel" and let it shine! If we embraced the cities with the evangelical fervor of the 16th-century Anabaptists – weeping over them, praying for them, evangelizing and serving them as Jesus did – we would have such an incredible collective transformation of heart and mind that the neighborhoods where we have planted all these new urban churches would also be transformed in the process! And then, as now, it would be the amazing grace of God using us perhaps in spite of rather than because of our centuries of cultural traditions. What a stretch for our old wineskins if we were to turn from a persecuted minority into a leavening majority!

Our collective history might suggest that we remain isolated and rural; our collective theology says we will love God and neighbor because Jesus meant what he said and we are naive enough to attempt – however imperfectly – to simply take him at his word, even in the city. Thomas Jefferson started a bad rumor when he called cities "pestilential cesspools of violence" which may, if unchecked, infect and destroy entire nations. There is certainly truth in his thesis, but he was selectively remembering Sodom and Gomorrah and forgetting the first murder in the Bible, which happened on a farm. Most Americans (and most Mennonites!) seem to have been infected with the Jeffersonian myopia, forgetting such wonderful biblical models as the cities of refuge, Nineveh repenting en masse, Jerusalem as God's and David's favorite hometown, the urban churches of the New Testament, and the New Jerusalem as God's resettlement plan. In order to see the future as God sees it, we need-in addition to our wonderfully-polished rural glasses to also begin peering through urban, suburban, and even regional glasses to gain a God's-eye perspective. God started human history in a garden, but he will end it in a city. We Mennonites need to rise up and follow.

Memorial Tribute for Dirck E. Stoltzfus
by Carol M. Marnet

I learned many things in my 17-year friendship with Dirck, but perhaps the most outstanding was Dirck's love of life. Despite his limitations, he determined that whatever he could do, he would do well. He not only did well, in many cases he did very well. His love of music and memorization of Scripture were an inspiration to all those he met.

During the Memorial service, Brother Raymond Jackson said that Dirck's house was built of silver as opposed to wood or straw. I agree with Raymond, but I think he left out an important ingredient of Dirck's being – that of love. Not only did Dirck love life, he loved people as well. This was evident in his genuine joy in greeting people, whether they were friends of long standing or newly made friends. It was also evident in what was one of his favorite phrases, "Make your mouth look happy; don't make your mouth look sad." Many times he gently but effectively reminded me that a Christian's life was to be one of joy and love, and was not to be bogged down with the cares of the world.

His life enriched mine by his prayers at Prayer Meeting, his delight and ability in drawing, his pleasure in the everyday aspects of life that many tend to overlook. Thank you for being my friend these last 17 years, Dirck. I shall be a better person for having known you.

Summer Bible School Memories
by Sadie Yost

Sadie Yost was a high school teacher at Lancaster Mennonite High School. She came to Diamond Street in the mid-fifties to teach summer Bible School (a four week affair in those days).

She taught the older students. The first day she was recording names. The first was "Mike". She wrote it down. The second was "Mike". She thought it strange but possible. After she had four or five "Mikes" she was sure they were pulling her leg. "Okay, now, what are your real names?"

Bible School was held in the morning at the church and then in the evening Alma Ruth and Emma Rudy held an open air Bible School. They went to a vacant lot and went up and down the streets nearby gathering children. Emma had a series of 10 verses that she taught – there were beautiful picture posters with a verse to match. Students recited to the helpers. If they said all 10 verses perfectly, they got a prize. One boy recited the given verse – "The righteous shall flourish like a palm tree; he shall grow like a cedar in Lebanon." The child said, "The righteous shall flourish like a palm tree; he shall grow like a seed in a lemon." Sadie said she counted it perfectly right.

Another time Sadie was helping in the preschool class. Sadie threatened a child who was misbehaving, "If you do that again, I'll have to hold you on my lap." He promptly repeated so she would hold him.

Sadie enjoyed the interaction with the children very much. One little guy enamoured her with his charms and she said to him, "You are so cute, I think I'll put you in my suitcase and take you along home with me." Another little fellow standing nearby said wistfully, "Do you have room in there for me, too?"

Memories
by Ruth (Eby) Gehman

Ruth helped with Bible School at Diamond Street several years. Also her church, Hershey's Mennonite, helped for many years to distribute *The Way*. They left from their church and drove with 2 or 3 cars to Diamond Street. They were met in the church by Like Stoltzfus who gave them directions of where to go. They went by 2's. When finished they returned home with good feelings and good stories.

Police and fire sirens blowing any time day and night, people talking, everyone hustling here and there, a covering of black soot, dirty streets, train whistles blowing, horns honking, men lying on the sidewalk in a drunken stupor, the elevated and subway cars clanking loudly, noise, noise, noise everywhere. Was this really to be my home for the next two years? Would I be able to make all the necessary adjustments? After all, I was a country farm girl. My life was lived with little challenge.

Now I was a new bride wanting so badly to meet my new husband's expectations. Tried to set up housekeeping with little furniture, climbed two flights of stairs, no bathtub or shower, hot, humid, mucky days. What had I gotten myself into? God knew exactly what he was doing. He knew I needed more challenges so stretching could happen. A few stretching experiences were teaching Sunday School and Summer Bible School and helping with girls club, a real challenge, even city driving was a challenge. I recall the day I had a doctor's appointment. Returning home I made a wrong turn. I was lost and it was getting dark. Needless to say I was frightened and upset. Finally I stopped to ask direction. There were lots of right and left turns to make and I couldn't remember all of them. I asked the Lord to please help me find my way home and he was faithful. I came to a stop sign and there was the street I knew. A big faith booster! God does care!

Lessons learned: I can't live on my own. I need the Lord's help to live in victory. There are committed Christians other than Mennonites, I didn't have all the answers after all, listening and ministering to people takes time, where there are people friends can be found. We did make many new friends in Philadelphia.

I found God's grace sufficient for the adjustment and challenges. It was a time of finding my own identity, making our own decisions away from family and church community, a time of soul searching to experience my security in Christ in a new light. Philadelphia was a very good three years and three months' experience. The challenges helped to mold and shape me into the person I am today. It was with some regret and sadness when we felt the Lord leading us out of the city to another chapter in our lives. We learned to enjoy city life and to love the people we cared about. We are thankful for the good and bad experiences. Our lives have been blessed and enriched and I have grown spiritually because of having been there.

– Ferne Lehman

My involvement with the Mennonite Church began the summer of 1961 when I attended Missionary Training Institute with my future wife, Ferne. Through God's leading, we accepted Jacob Frederick's invitation to move into the third floor apartment at Norris Square Church and assist in the program of the congregation. After our marriage in November, we moved to Philadelphia and I began serving my two years of alternative services at the Episcopal Hospital. Three years of city living was life changing for this country boy. Moving from the farm to the city, from single to married life, new job and a new church required adjustments that were not easy. After many weeks of being on an emotional roller coaster, the Lord graciously shone His light into the dark night of my soul and began emotional and spiritual restoration.

Participation in Sunday School, Summer Bible School, outdoor park meetings and door to door visitation provided opportunities for personal growth. I well remember the first Sunday of teaching a boys class. In a grand attempt to make connections with the boys, I extended an open invitation to visit my wife and I. To my wife's surprise and dismay, several hungry boys appeared at our apartment for lunch that very day. Another fond memory was fellowshipping with the brothers and sisters at Diamond Street Church. I recall an experience of washing the feet of a dear black brother and the washing away of racial prejudice as he washed my feet in return. One of the highlights of our time in the city was the missionary training institute held each summer at the Norris Square Church facility. The teaching sessions and fellowship with the participants were so refreshing.

Relating to city youth and their culture was a real challenge. It was frustrating to watch youth accept Christ and become members of the church only to eventually leave again. Why could they not remain faithful to Christ? It was a time of soul searching. The Lord began teaching me that Christianity is more than an external code of ethics. It is a matter of the heart, a personal relationship with our heavenly Father. My involvement with the mission of the church in Philadelphia was a time of testing my belief systems and convictions. God put a desire in my heart that continues to the present time, to know and experience Christ and daily live for His Glory.

– Marcus Lehman

ENDNOTES

[1] Ross L. Bender. 1986. "It was large and fancy". *The Mennonite*. 101: 9

[2] Wenger, A. Grace. 1989. "Women in Mission in Lancaster". *Missionary Messenger*. October.

[3] Good, Robert W. 1995. "Origins of the Diamond Street Mennonite Church in Philadelphia, Pennsylvania: 1942 to 1967". *Pennsylvania Mennonite Heritage*. April. XVIII (2): 16-25.

[4] Greiser, David. 1993. "The Mennonites of Philadelphia: When church begets church begets church". *Gospel Herald*. June 15, 22, & 29th. 86 (24-26).

[5] For a comprehensive description of the first Mennonite settlements in America, see Richard K. MacMaster, *Land, Piety, Peoplehood: The Establishment of Mennonite Communities in America, 1683-1790*. The Mennonite Experience in America, volume one, Scottdale, PA and Kitchener, Ont.: Herald Press.

[6] See Ross L. Bender. 1986. "It was large and fancy". *The Mennonite*. 101: 9 for a more complete overview of First Mennonite and Second Mennonite Church.

[7] See Juhnke (1989) for more detailed description of the relationship between the World's Fair and Chicago mission development. Juhnke, James. 1989. *Vision, Doctrine, War: Mennonite Identity and Organization in America, 1890-1930*. Scottdale, PA: Herald Press.

[8] From Department of Justice, Immigration and Naturalization Service, Annual Reports. Acquired in Ahlstrom (1972).

[9] Juhnke, James. Pg. 156. 1989. *Vision, Doctrine, War: Mennonite Identity and Organization in America, 1890-1930*. Scottdale, PA: Herald Press.

[10] A different denomination from the Eastern District of the General Conference Mennonite Church mentioned above.

[11] "Proceedings of the Franconia Conference, 1880-1907," p. 13, unpublished translation by Raymond Hollenbach of minutes by Jacob D. Mensch, Mennonite Historians of Eastern Pennsylvania, Harleysville, PA. From Good (1995).

[12] See Wenger, A. Grace. 1989. "Women in Mission in Lancaster". *Missionary Messenger*. September.

[13] From Wenger, A. Grace. 1989. "Women in Mission in Lancaster". *Missionary Messenger*. September.

[14] These included the Galen Martin family, the Jim and Beth Leaman family, and the Freeman Miller family.

[15] See Roy Burkholder. 1997. "J. Paul Graybill, the Progressive Conservative" in *Be Not Conformed to the World* Morgantown, PA: Masthoff Press.

[16] See Wenger, A. Grace. 1989. "Women in Mission in Lancaster". *Missionary Messenger*. September.

[17] See *Missionary Messenger*. July 15, 1927.

[18] This story was written by J. Paul Graybill - "The Bromley Family", February 9, 1938. Lancaster Mennonite Historical Society Box - Norris Square - J. Paul Graybill's addition. folder - J. Paul Graybill correspondence (Norris Square). .

[19] Earnestine Agnew presently lives at Landis Homes and enjoys the continuing spiritual nurture she receives there. She was in the baptismal class of 1927.

[20] "Data on Philadelphia Mission". February 18, 1937. Lancaster Mennonite Historical Society.

[21] Personal Diary of Emma Rudy.

[22] Eastern Mennonite Board of Missions and Charities, Minutes of Quarterly Meeting, April 12, 1935.

[23] Eastern Mennonite Board of Missions and Charities, Minutes of Quarterly Meeting, June 14, 1930 reports that Graybill "very much needed a rest".

[24] Eastern Mennonite Board of Missions and Charities, Minutes of Quarterly Meeting, March 29, 1936.

[25] Interview with Fred Yocum. September 29, 1999.

[26] Martha taught Sunday School and Clayton was a trustee and church treasurer. Jacob and Isaac, their sons, became Christians at Norris Square and along with Rebecca, their daughter, taught Sunday School, Summer Bible School, did street evangelism, and youth activities. Isaac was later ordained for ministry in Florida and served in Honduras and Christian education at Eastern Mennonite High School in Harrisonburg, Virginia and Lancaster Mennonite High School in Pennsylvania.

[27] Written correspondence with Wilmer Hollinger.

[28] Minutes from a Philadelphia Mennonite Pastor's meeting - February 29, 1960. Lancaster Mennonite Historical Society.

[29] Letter from Ruth (no last name) to J. Paul Graybill. No date. Lancaster Mennonite Historical Society.

[30] Personal reflections of Jim Leaman - 1999.

[31] "Mennonite Mission for the Colored" - hardbound book in "Diamond Street Congregation" box at Lancaster Mennonite Historical Society. Entry on October 20, 1935.

[32] "Mennonite Mission for the Colored" - hardbound book in "Diamond Street Congregation" box at Lancaster Mennonite Historical Society. Entry on October 29, 1935.

[33] Good, Robert W. 1995. "Origins of the Diamond Street Mennonite Church in Philadelphia, Pennsylvania: 1942 to 1967". *Pennsylvania Mennonite Heritage*. April. XVIII (2): 16-25.

[34] "Mennonite Mission for the Colored" - hardbound book in "Diamond Street Congregation" box at Lancaster Mennonite Historical Society. Entry on July 1937.

[35] "Mennonite Mission for the Colored" - hardbound book in "Diamond Street Congregation" box at Lancaster Mennonite Historical Society. Entry on November 27, 1938.

[36] From notes from the 40th Anniversary service of Diamond Street Mennonite Church. Unknown author. Located at Lancaster Mennonite Historical Society in box "Emma Rudy - 1953-63-66-74 - Historical and Commemorative Notes".

[37] Interview with Luke Stoltzfus, January 6, 1998.

[38] Personal correspondence with Homer Schrock.

[39] Interview with Mattie Nikiema, April 13, 1998.

[40] Philadelphia Missions Survey Report, April 2-4, 1956. Written by Ira J. Buckwalter and H. Raymond Charles. Lancaster Mennonite Historical Society.

[41] Review of Philadelphia Mission Program. December 4, 1962. Lancaster Mennonite Historical Library.

[42] Personal correspondence with Jim Leaman.

[43] Personal correspondence with Jim Leaman.

[44] See *Living Waters*, an autobiographical account written by Ruth Graybill, for an interesting and thorough description of much of the Mennonite ministry to Jews in the 20th century.

[45] Kniss, Fred. Pg. 64. 1997. *Disquiet in the Land: Cultural Conflict and American Mennonite Communities*. New Brunswick, NJ: Rutgers University Press.

[46] For a comprehensive review of the post-1965 "new immigration" in the U.S., see Douglas S. Massey, "The New Immigration and Ethnicity in the United States". *Population and Development Review*. 21 (3). 1995.

[47] Stoltzfus, Luke. 1973. "Planning for Mennonite Church Growth from a Sociological Perspective". Lancaster Mennonite Historical Society.

[48] Interview with Lemuel So, August 16, 1999.

[49] See "Fighting Like Heaven" by Charles Bulford in *Missionary Messenger*. April 1999. Also, "Charles and Nadine Smith: A ghost of a chance", by Kathleen Hayes in *Christian Living*, July-August 1995.

[50] Personal interview with Jacob Frederick

Lancaster Conference Philadelphia District Mennonite Pastors

Norris Square Mennonite Church
J. Paul Graybill (1922-1939)
Clarence Fretz (1940-1951)
Jacob Frederick (1951-1971)
Jim Leaman (1971-1974)

Diamond Street Mennonite Church
Clinton Ferster (1942-1943)
J. Harold Brenneman (1946-1950)
Frank Garman (1950-1951)
Luke Stoltzfus (1951-1965)
Homer Schrock (1965-1970)
Raymond Jackson (1970-1974)
Roy Newswanger (1974-1975)
Freeman Miller (1975-1987)
Charles Baynard (1987-1996)
Otis Banks (1996-present)

Oxford Circle Mennonite Church
John Winter (1952-1958)
     *ordained in '52 but started in '49
Donald Wenger (1957-1962)
Stoner Krady (1962-1966)
George Weber (1966-1971)
Jacob Frederick (1971-1972)
Kenneth Bucher (1972-1977)
James Leaman (1977-1998)
Vandy Parks, interim (1998-1999)
Leonard Dow (1999-present)

Arca de Salvacion
(dates not available)
Eugenio Matos
Benjamin Perez
Isadoro Saez
Arcadio and Matilda Tolentino
Diodoro Baez
Juan Carmona

Bethany House of Worship
Sanjeevaro Vangore (1980-present)

Vietnamese Mennonite Church
Quang Tran (1982-present)

Love Truth Chinese Mennonite Church
Lemuel So (1988-present)
Sing Kin So (1999-present)

Abundant Life Chinese Mennonite Church
Ted Yao (1987-1988)
Philip Dich (1988-1994)
Truong Tu (1994-present)

Philadelphia Cambodian Mennonite Church
Ted Yao (1989-1990)
Luke Stoltzfus (1990-1992)
Sarin Lay (1992-present)

Salam Mennonite Fellowship
George Kuttab (1989-present)

Christian Life Mennonite Church
Parker Mavi (1990-1992)
James Dennis (1993-present)

Ethiopian Evangelical Fellowship
Yeshitela Mengistu (1990-1995)
Tesfaye Satargie (1997-present)

New Mercies Mennonite Church
Charles and Nadine Smith-Bulford (1993-present)

Kapatiran Christian Church
Ton Alcantara (1996-present)

Way of Life Ministries
Duane and Pam Royster (1998-present)

List of long-term Lancaster Conference "sister workers" in Philadelphia
Amanda Musselman
     (Norris Square): 1899-1924
Mary Denlinger
     (Norris Square): 1899-1924
Barbara Herr
     (Norris Square): 1926-1955
Kathryn Hess
     (Norris Square): 1946-1956
Emma Rudy
     (Norris Square & Diamond Street): 1926-1961
Alma Ruth
     (Diamond Street): 1942-1961
Laura Weber
     (Oxford Circle): 1949-1977
Esther Clark
     (Oxford Circle): 1950-1987

Index of Names